Contracts for Independent Readers

Realistic Fiction

Grades 4–6

Writers:
Dee Benson, Colleen Dabney, Rusty Fischer, Michael Foster, Kimberly Minafo,
Lori Sammartino, David Webb

Editors:
Kim T. Griswell and Cayce Guiliano

Contributing Editors:
Deborah T. Kalwat and Mary Lester

Art Coordinator:
Donna K. Teal

Artists:
Nick Greenwood, Clevell Harris, Sheila Krill, Mary Lester, Kimberly Richard,
Greg D. Rieves, Rebecca Saunders, Donna K. Teal

Cover Artist:
Nick Greenwood

www.themailbox.com

©2001 by THE EDUCATION CENTER, INC.
All rights reserved.
ISBN #1-56234-409-9

Manufactured in the United States

10 9 8 7 6 5 4 3 2 1

Table of Contents

About This Book

What is realistic fiction?

Realistic fiction contains events that could possibly happen in real life but that may not actually have occurred. The characters in realistic fiction can be fictional as long as they behave in realistic ways. The main characters are usually involved in a dilemma or conflict that is resolved as the plot develops.

How to use this book:

Contracts for Independent Readers—Realistic Fiction includes everything you will need to implement an independent reading program in your classroom.

The **Teacher's Organizational Checklist** on page 4 will help you monitor your students' progress throughout the year. To use this page, photocopy it to make a class supply and write each student's name in the space provided. Hold a conference with each student to assess the goals the student has for the semester or the year. Have the student write her goals in the space provided. Next, have each student choose one of the novels included in this book to read. List the title of the book in the appropriate column. When the student has completed an activity, write the date it was completed in the bottom portion of the corresponding box. Use the key at the bottom of the page to note the type of activity completed in the top portion of the corresponding box as shown in the sample. After evaluating the activities, write any comments you have in the space provided and have the student do the same. At the end of the semester or year, direct each student to complete the self-assessment portion detailing how she feels she has done at reaching her goals. Finally, write your own assessment of each student's progress.

The **introductory page** of each independent contract contains a description of the novel, background information on the author, and a student contract materials list. This list will aid you in preparing in advance any materials that students may need. Most of the listed materials can be found right in the classroom!

Each of the two programmable **contract pages** in each unit has six independent activities for students to choose from. Each unit also includes **reproducible pages** that correspond to several independent activities. The second contract page has slightly more advanced activities than the first contract page.

Since some novels are at higher reading levels or may contain more mature content, we suggest that you read each of the novels so that you may assist students in choosing which novels to read.

Also included in this book is a **student booklist** on page 61, which consists of 12 realistic fiction novels with a brief description of each. This list provides you with additional titles for students who finish early, for students who would enjoy reading other books in this genre, and for you to include in your classroom library.

Other Books in the Contracts for Independent Readers Series:
- *Contracts for Independent Readers—Historical Fiction*
- *Contracts for Independent Readers—Humor*
- *Contracts for Independent Readers—Fantasy*
- *Contracts for Independent Readers—Mystery*
- *Contracts for Independent Readers—Adventure*

Book Title

Student Comments

Teacher Comments

Sample: Book Title

Activity 1 | Activity 2 | Activity 3 | Activity 4 | Activity 5 | Activity 6 | Activity 7 | Activity 8 | Activity 9 | Activity 10 | Activity 11 | Activity 12

| MA | SS | | | LA | | | | | | |
| 11/6 | 11/7 | | | 11/10 | | | | | | |

Student Goals:

Self-Assessment:

Teacher Assessment:

Key
LA = Language Arts
RD = Reading
W = Writing
MA = Math
SS = Social Studies
SC = Science
A = Art
MU = Music
RS = Research
CT = Critical Thinking

Bridge to Terabithia

by Katherine Paterson

About the Book

Jess Aarons's new neighbor Leslie Burke is different from the other girls at school. She wears cutoffs and a blue undershirt instead of a prim dress. She crosses over to the boys' side of the playground and outruns Jess in a race he's been practicing for all summer. Despite Leslie's differences, the two become inseparable. Together, they create the secret kingdom of Terabithia, where they reign as king and queen. They fight off imaginary foes and help each other through the trials of adolescence. But one tragic day, Leslie drowns trying to swing across the river on the rope that takes them to Terabithia. As Jess deals with his grief, he realizes that Leslie has helped "push back the walls of his mind and make him see beyond to the shining world." He knows that her friendship has changed him forever.

About the Author

Katherine Paterson was born on October 31, 1932, in China and spent part of her childhood there. She was in China in 1937 when war broke out between China and Japan, and feels that the experiences of war and all the moving her family did helped shape who she is and the kind of books she writes.

Students will appreciate knowing that Paterson never wanted to be a writer growing up. When she was ten, she wanted to be a movie star or a missionary. At 20, she wanted to get married and have lots of children. Paterson wrote her first novel while taking an adult education class with a friend.

Now Paterson lives with her family in Barre, Vermont. She says she loves writing and is "spoiled" to be able to work at home in her study. She can wear whatever she wants, she never has to call in sick, and she gets to visit schools and meet delightful people. Her writing has been honored with many awards, including the Newbery Medal.

Student Contract Materials List

- Activity #1: construction paper, ruler, crayons or markers
- Activity #2: shoebox, crayons or markers, craft supplies, index card
- Activity #3: construction paper, markers
- Activity #4: song lyrics, 3 sheets of construction paper, crayons or markers
- Activity #5: newspaper (obituary section)
- Activity #6: copy of page 8
- Activity #7: copy of page 9

- Activity #8: reference materials on Washington, DC; construction paper; crayons or markers
- Activity #9: paper, pencil
- Activity #10: reference materials on flooding, construction paper, crayons or markers
- Activity #11: crayons or markers, construction paper
- Activity #12: copy of page 10

Bridge to Terabithia
Independent Contract

Name:_____ Number of activities to be completed: _____

1. Math

Jess is a terrific artist, but lacks courage. Leslie is a great runner, but doesn't fit in. What are the students in your class best at? Worst at? Write two survey questions to help you find out. Ask the questions of at least 15 class-mates and tally the results. Next, graph the results and display them for all to see.

2. Art

Terabithia is a special place for Leslie and Jess. If you could create a fantasy place of your own, what would it be like? Using a shoebox, create a diorama of your secret place. It might be a tree house or a corner of a friend's garage. Think carefully about where it is, what materials you would use to create it, when you might go there, and who might go there with you. Then give your special place a name. On an index card, write the name of your special place and a paragraph describing what makes it special to you. Attach the index card to your diorama.

3. Social Studies

In chapter 4, Jess talks about Leslie's "mask of perfection." This is the side of Leslie that she lets her teachers see. Jess knows Leslie has many other sides. Using construction paper and markers, create Leslie's imaginary "mask of perfection." On the front, write an adjective to describe Leslie when she wears this mask. On the back, write about where and why she might act this way. Then use the events in the book to create a second mask that shows a different side of Leslie. Label this as you have done the first. As you work, think about the make-believe masks you wear each day.

4. Music

Ask your teacher for recordings or songbooks that feature the lyrics to some of the songs Miss Edmunds sings with her classes (see chapter 2). Or ask a parent or teacher to help you use the Internet to locate lyrics. Find lyrics that you think would be meaningful to Jess. Then find lyrics that would be meaningful to Leslie. Do the same for Janice Avery. On each of three sheets of construction paper, draw one of the characters singing. Draw a conver-sation bubble next to each character. In each bubble, write the lyrics you think each charac-ter would want to sing.

5. Writing

After Leslie's death, Jess begins to remember all of the things that have made her special. When someone dies, the local newspaper will usually print an obituary telling about the person's death and giving some details about the person's life. Take a look at the obituary section in your local newspaper. Consider the types of information that have been presented. Now pretend you are Jess and you've been asked to write Leslie's obituary for the local newspaper. Think about Leslie's abilities, family, and life history, as well as the friendship you have shared. Then write an obituary to share the information with others.

6. Language Arts

A simile is a phrase that uses *like* or *as* to compare two different things. Obtain a copy of page 8 from your teacher. After reading the examples of similes given, look through the book to find additional examples to help your vocabulary branch out.

Bridge to Terabithia
Independent Contract

Name:_____ Number of activities to be completed: _____

7. ## Writing

Jess admires the way Leslie can use words to describe things or tell about her feelings. He is better at finding the right words after a situation has ended. Obtain a copy of page 9 from your teacher and see whether you can find the right words to write.

8. ## Social Studies

In chapter 10, Jess and Miss Edmunds go to the National Gallery in Washington, DC. Research to find out more about the National Gallery and any two of the other places mentioned in chapter 10. Then write and illustrate a travel brochure about Washington, DC, that highlights the places you have researched.

9. ## Reading

Authors sometimes use a recurring image to symbolize a theme in a story. In *Bridge to Terabithia,* one recurring image is falling. Find at least three examples of the author's use of falling in the book. Write a description of each example and note the pages on which it is found. Then write what you think falling means in the story. Are the characters really falling? Are they going somewhere? Or are they changing in some way?

10. ## Science

In the beginning of the story, the creek bed is dry. Then Jess describes it changing into a "roaring eight-foot-wide sea." How could it change like that? Research flash floods. Divide a piece of construction paper into three sections. In the first section, draw pictures and write a short explanation of what causes a flood. In the second section, draw pictures and write a description of the kind of damage a flash flood can cause. In the third section, list things people should do to keep safe during a flood.

11. ## Reading

Bill and Judy Burke are writers. Imagine that they decide to dedicate their next three books to Leslie. What might the titles be? What would each book be about? Design a dust jacket for each book, featuring the title, the Author, a summary of the book, and an "About the Author" section. Use what you have learned about Bill and Judy in chapter 4 and throughout the book to complete the task.

12. ## Writing

In chapter 10, Jess smiles as he thinks about getting a "gut transplant." This, he imagines, would give him instant courage. Consider the things you'd like to be better at. Wouldn't it be neat if you could get a transplant to help you improve a weakness? What kind of a transplant would you get? Pretend that you get the transplant you wish for. Obtain a copy of page 10 from your teacher to help you write and illustrate a newspaper story describing the result of your transplant.

Bridge to Terabithia

Branching Out With Similes!

Study the examples of similes below. Then look through _Bridge to Terabithia_ to find additional examples of similes. Write an example and the page on which it is found in each leaf.

The boys quivered on the edges of their seats like moths fighting to be freed of co-coons. (p. 24)

Momma would be mad as flies in a fruit jar. (p.1)

©2001 The Education Center, Inc. • _Contracts for Independent Readers_ • _Realistic Fiction_ • TEC789

Note to the teacher: Use with activity #6 on page 6.

The Write Words

Unlike Leslie, Jess sometimes has a hard time thinking of what he wants to say at the time he wants to say it. Sometimes, writing helps us carefully consider what we want to say without being pressured to think quickly. On the back of this page or on another sheet of paper, write responses to any two of the situations below.

After their perfect day together, Jess is unable to thank Miss Edmunds in the way he wants. Pretend you are Jess and write a letter to her, thoughtfully thanking her for your day together. Include examples of things you did, how you felt, and what the day meant to you.

Imagine you are Janice Avery. Write about one of the events in the book in your diary. You might choose the afternoon of Jess and Leslie's trick, the day Leslie talks to you about what has happened with your dad, or when you find out Leslie has died.

Imagine you are May Belle and you've just been hit by Jess (chapter 12). Write him a note telling him how you feel about being hit and how you feel about Leslie's dying. Remember that you are only six years old.

In chapter 13, Jess considers writing a letter to Mrs. Myers, telling her that Leslie thought she was a great teacher. Pretend you are Jess and write the letter.

Jess is unable to thank Leslie for the paints in the way he wants to. Use watercolors to decorate a thank-you card for her. Pretending you are Jess, write a thank-you note inside the card.

After Leslie dies, Jess wants to know that Bill doesn't blame him for anything. But he doesn't know how to ask such a sensitive question. Pretend you are Jess, just after you have crowned May Belle the new queen of Terabithia. Write Bill a letter telling him what Leslie has meant to you and ask him whether he blames you in any way for Leslie's death.

Jess's dad never really says much to him. What do you think he would say to Jess if he could find the words? Pretend you are Mr. Aarons and write a letter telling Jess all that is on your mind.

Note to the teacher: Use with activity #7 on page 7.

Read All About It!

In *Bridge to Terabithia,* Jess wants a gut transplant to help him cope with his fears. What type of transplant would help you with a problem you have? Use the graphic organizer below to help you plan a newspaper article about your transplant. Then write and illustrate the article on the blank newspaper page provided.

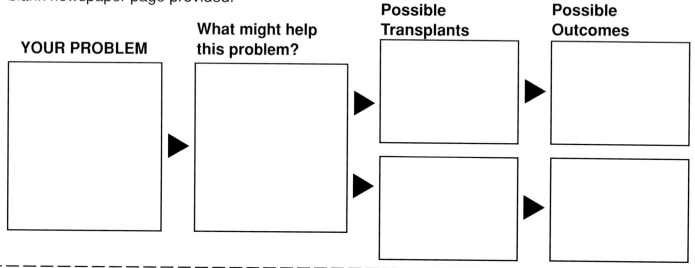

YOUR PROBLEM

What might help this problem?

Possible Transplants

Possible Outcomes

LOCAL STUDENT RECEIVES TRANSPLANT, SAYS LIFE IS DIFFERENT NOW!

_____ _____
          city   state

Reported by _____

_____

_____

_____

_____

_____

_____

_____

_____

_____

_____

_____

_____

Harriet the Spy
by Louise Fitzhugh

About the Book

Eleven-year-old Harriet M. Welsch is going to be a writer when she grows up, so she spies on people and writes down everything she sees. Her best friends, Sport and Janie, know that she writes down observations in her notebook. What they don't know is that she writes about them as well. Harriet's notes are brutally honest descriptions of her observations and her feelings about what she sees. When Harriet drops her spy notebook and her friends read what she has written about them, the trouble begins. Harriet is left out of the group and feels utterly alone. Not even her beloved nurse, Ole Golly, can help her, and Harriet's parents don't know what to do with her. She's starting to wonder if she'll ever get her friends back.

About the Author

Louise Fitzhugh was born in Memphis, Tennessee, on October 5, 1928. She was an only child and lived with her father. Louise was writing by age 11. She went to an elite school, Miss Hutchinson's School, until college. She attended several colleges before enrolling at the Art Students League and then Cooper Union. Fitzhugh's primary interest for years was art, but she continued to write. In her first published book, she was listed as the illustrator—not the author.

At age 35, Fitzhugh began writing *Harriet the Spy*. This is the book she is most remembered for. She wrote other less-famous books, such as *Nobody's Family Is Going to Change* and *The Long Secret* (the sequel to *Harriet the Spy*). Unfortunately, Fitzhugh died at the age of 46 from an aneurysm, just one week before *Nobody's Family* was published.

Student Contract Materials List

- Activity #1: paper, pencil
- Activity #2: tape recorder, blank tape
- Activity #3: 1 sheet of 9" x 12" light-colored construction paper, crayons or markers
- Activity #4: paper, pencil
- Activity #5: copy of page 14
- Activity #6: index cards, string, hole puncher, crayons or markers
- Activity #7: science project board, crayons or markers
- Activity #8: copy of page 15
- Activity #9: tape recorder, blank tape; or paper, pencil
- Activity #10: paper, pencil
- Activity #11: reference materials on different dances
- Activity #12: copy of page 16

Harriet the Spy
Independent Contract

Name:_____   Number of activities to be completed: _____

 1. **Writing**

Harriet writes blunt descriptions of people she knows and sees each day on her spy route. Improve your descriptive writing by keeping a people journal of your own. Write your impressions of the people you see each day. Try to keep your descriptions honest, but positive. Keep your journal for at least a week, making notes each day.

 2. **Music**

Pretend you have been asked to write the theme song of a new TV show based on *Harriet the Spy*. Think of a catchy refrain and add verses or change the words to one of your favorite songs. Try to capture the spirit of the book in the words, the rhythm, and the tune of your song. Then record your song and play it for the class.

 3. **Art**

Louise Fitzhugh drew her own illustrations for *Harriet the Spy*. Pretend you are an artist hired by a publishing company to draw a new cover and illustrations for an anniversary edition of the book. Choose at least three of your favorite scenes and draw a sketch for each one. Then draw a new cover illustration. Share the book with the class, showing your illustrations and new cover.

 4. **Writing**

Harriet wants to be a spy so she will know everything there is to know. If you could be a spy anywhere in the world during any time in history, where and when would you choose? Write a tale about your spying adventures in your chosen place and time. Include how you will get to this place, what you will attempt to discover while you are there, the dangerous details about your discovery attempts, and how you will get the information back home safely.

 5. **Language Arts**

Harriet gets into trouble for the things she says about people in her notebook. How would you apologize if the same thing happened to you? Obtain a copy of page 14 from your teacher and practice your apologizing skills.

 6. **Language Arts**

Harriet uses simple tools to spy on people, such as a notebook, a pen, and a flashlight. Since this book was written, there have been many inventions that could make spying easier. Make a list of inventions that you would find helpful in the spy game, such as the Internet and minicameras. Create an eight-page booklet of spy equipment by writing the name of each invention at the top of an index card and then writing a sentence explaining how to use the invention for spying. Draw a picture of each invention on the corresponding card. Bind your book together by punching a hole in the upper left-hand corner of each card, stacking the cards, and tying a string through the holes.

Harriet the Spy

Independent Contract

Name:_____ Number of activities to be completed: _____

7. Science

Harriet's friend Janie is a budding scientist and inventor. Imagine what kind of experiment she might have demonstrated at her school science fair. Create a science fair display for an imaginary potion that does something wonderful and amazing, such as making the wearer of the potion a perfect speller or a math wiz. Use the scientific method to show each step in Janie's process, including her observations when testing it on friends or relatives.

8. Math

Sport is responsible for keeping track of his family's finances. Obtain a copy of page 15 from your teacher to find out whether you can calculate your own expenses.

9. Social Studies

In the book, Italian immigrants operate their own store in the city. What types of challenges face people who immigrate to the United States? Talk to your family and find out what country or countries your ancestors came from. Choose one relative who immigrated here and interview him or her. If you are not able to interview this person, ask other family members what life was like for him or her after moving here. Was learning the language difficult? Was it hard to get a job? Tape-record your interview or write your questions and the interviewee's answers. Share your findings with the class.

10. Language Arts

Harriet has her own spy route that she follows each day after school. Buy or make a spy notebook. Then map out a spy route in your neighborhood. Jog or walk along your route at least five times at different times of the day and on different days. Pay attention to as many details as you can each time you go. When you get home, write down in your spy notebook whom you saw, what you saw, and your thoughts about each person or thing.

11. Social Studies

In chapter 5, Harriet must learn to dance. Find a book in the library that contains the steps to the cotillion, square dancing, or another form of dance that you do not already know. Learn the steps to the dance and practice it until you feel confident enough to teach several members of your class. Then hold a small dance class with you as the teacher.

12. Critical Thinking

The thoughts Harriet writes down range from concern to criticism. It is easy to tell who each person she describes is because her notes clearly define the faults and differences of each one. Obtain a copy of page 16 from your teacher to find out which people Harriet is talking about.

14

Apologies Aplenty

Have you ever said or written something about someone that you later regretted? Follow the directions below to help Harriet apologize to her friends and classmates for the things she wrote about them in her notebook.

Directions: Read each quote below. Pretend you are Harriet and you want to apologize for what you wrote. On the back of this sheet or on another sheet of paper, write an apology to each person for the mean things that you wrote.

"Maybe Beth Ellen doesn't have any parents. I asked her her mother's name and she couldn't remember. She said she had only seen her once and she didn't remember it very well. She wears strange things like orange sweaters and a big black car comes for her once a week and she goes someplace else."

"What to do about Pinky Whitehead: 1. Turn the hose on him. 2. Pinch his ears until he screams. 3. Tear his pants off and laugh at him."

"If Marion Hawthorne doesn't watch out she's going to grow up into a lady Hitler."

"If Laura Peters doesn't stop smiling at me in that wishy-washy way I'm going to give her a good kick."

"Who does Janie Gibbs think she's kidding? Does she really think she could ever be a scientist?"

"Today a new boy arrived. He is so dull no one can remember his name so I have named him the Boy with the Purple Socks. Where would he imagine. Where would he ever find purple socks?"

"Sometimes I can't stand Sport. With his worrying all the time and fussing over his and fussing over his father, sometimes he's like a little old woman."

©2001 The Education Center, Inc. • Contracts for Independent Readers • Realistic Fiction • TEC789

Note to the teacher: Use with activity #5 on page 12.

Budgeting Basics

Where does all the money go? Keep track of your budget by following the directions below.
Directions: Fill in the top of the chart (Expenses) with the things you spend money on, such as clothes, movies, video games, and sodas or snacks. Under each expense, list the amount of money you spend on each item each day for two weeks. Then add your expenses to discover how much you spend per item.

Expenses:					Other
Monday					
Tuesday					
Wednesday					
Thursday					
Friday					
Saturday					
Sunday					
Monday					
Tuesday					
Wednesday					
Thursday					
Friday					
Saturday					
Sunday					
TOTALS:					

Use the totals above to complete each chart below.

Pie Chart Divide the pie to show the amount each of your expenses takes away from your allowance. **Hint:** Larger expenses get larger pieces of the pie, and smaller expenses get smaller pieces.

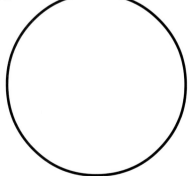

Bar Graph Complete the bar graph by adding your expenses from above and then graphing the amount of money spent on each.

Are you spending your money wisely? After seeing how much money you spend on each item, will you change your spending habits? Will you start saving more of your money? Explain.

_____

Guess Who!

The following passages are from Harriet's notebook, except the names of those being described have been left out. Can you tell whom each passage is about? Write each person's name in the space provided. Then draw a picture of the person based on the description and what you know about the person from the book.

1. Sometimes he "looks as though he's been up all night. He has funny little dry things around his eyes. I worry about him."	**2.** "She's so dull if I was her I couldn't stand myself."	**3.** She "has brown eyes and brown hair. Her hands wiggle around a lot. She frowns when she looks at things close."
_____	_____	_____
4. Her "feet look larger this year." She "has buck teeth, thin hair, feet like skis, and a very long hanging stomach."	**5.** He "has not changed. He will never change."	**6.** She "gets stranger every year. I think she <u>might</u> blow up the world."
_____	_____	_____

Maniac Magee
by Jerry Spinelli

About the Book

After Jeffrey Magee's parents are killed in a tragic accident when he is three years old, he goes to live with his aunt and uncle. The two of them are too busy ignoring each other to pay attention to him. So one day, in the middle of a school performance, he takes off running. He begins a life of wandering from place to place, searching for an address of his own—a place to call home. Eventually, he runs into Two Mills, a racially divided town, where blacks stay on the East End and whites stay on the West End. Soon, Jeffrey begins to make a name for himself as someone who performs fantastic feats—a real "maniac." Jeffrey "Maniac" Magee tries to settle into a caring home, first with the Beales, a family in the East End, and then with Mr. Grayson, an elderly baseball–park hand who lives in the West End. But Maniac must overcome his fears of abandonment and the town's prejudices before he can find a place to call home.

About the Author

Jerry Spinelli was born in 1941 in Norristown, Pennsylvania. When he was 16, his high school football team won a major victory, inspiring him to write a poem about it. When the poem was published in a local paper, he immediately dreamed of becoming a writer. First he tried writing novels for adults, but none of them sold. Then he decided to write for children. His first book, *Space Station Seventh Grade,* was published in 1982. Using his own memories as well as observing the children around him, he continued writing, and in 1991, he won the Newbery Medal for *Maniac Magee.* Of his more than 15 books for children, many have won recognition—making him one of the most popular writers of children's fiction.

Student Contract Materials List

- Activity #1: copy of page 20
- Activity #2: shoebox, glue, scissors, construction paper, various art supplies
- Activity #3: 4 sheets of drawing paper; crayons, markers, or colored pencils
- Activity #4: 12" x 18" sheet of white construction paper, markers, various art supplies
- Activity #5: reference materials on the Gordian knot
- Activity #6: 1 box of 64 crayons, one 12" x 18" sheet of white construction paper

- Activity #7: paper, pencil
- Activity #8: encyclopedia
- Activity #9: ten 4" x 6" index cards, reference materials on the civil rights movement, tape
- Activity #10: 10 sheets of construction paper, glue, ball of string
- Activity #11: copy of page 21
- Activity #12: one 10" x 14" sheet of white drawing paper, crayons or colored pencils

Maniac Magee
Independent Contract

Name:_____ Number of activities to be completed: _____

1. Reading

During his search for a home, Maniac lives in many different places. Obtain a copy of page 20 from your teacher. Using details from the book, write about two events that happen in each of Maniac's homes.

2. Art

Maniac feels at home in many different places, but he likes some places better than others. Create a shoebox replica of a place that you think Maniac would consider the home of his dreams. Use construction paper and other art materials to decorate Maniac's home with furniture and other items. Use facts from the story to help you decide what to include (for example, Maniac probably wouldn't want a bed).

3. Language Arts

Maniac's sneakers help make him into a legend. Choose four other characters from the story and design shoes for each. What kind of shoes would fit each character's life and personality? Running shoes? Baseball shoes? Work boots? On a separate sheet of paper, write the name of each character, draw a picture of his or her shoes, and then write a short paragraph stating why these shoes would fit that character.

4. Social Studies

Most of the story describes five seasons of Maniac Magee's life in Two Mills. Draw a timeline marking off five equal sections. Starting with "First Summer," label each section in order on the timeline: "First Summer," "First Fall," "First Winter," "First Spring," and "Second Summer." From the story, find several events that happen in each season. Illustrate and label each event in the corresponding section. Use the supplies provided by your teacher to add seasonal art in each section. Title your timeline "Maniac's First Year."

5. Research

Cobble's Knot is almost as famous in Two Mills as the Gordian knot was in ancient Greece. Research the Gordian knot. Then make a T-chart to compare and contrast the two knots. Draw a large T-chart on a piece of paper. Label the left side "Gordian knot" and the right side "Cobble's knot." List comparing and contrasting facts about each. Include where the knots came from, what made them so difficult to undo, who untied them, how the knots were untied, and what the people received for untying the knots.

6. Critical Thinking

Maniac could not understand how people could be referred to simply as "black" or "white" when they were all different shades and colors. Investigate the different shades of skin color by drawing two large outlines of a hand and arm. Find crayon colors that match each skin tone on your arm and hand. Color one of the outlines to match your skin tones, and write your name above it. Color and label the second outline to match the skin tones of a friend or family member. At the bottom of the sheet, write a paragraph telling how many colors you used and explaining why you agree or disagree with Maniac.

©2001 The Education Center, Inc. • *Contracts for Independent Readers • Realistic Fiction • TEC789*

Maniac Magee

Independent Contract

Name:_____ Number of activities to be completed: _____

Reading

Maniac's goal throughout the story is to find a real home. Draw a chart with four columns. Label the first column "Chapter," the second "Forward," the third "Backward," and the fourth "No Action." Refer to each chapter and write down the chapter number in the "Chapter" column. From the chapter's events, determine if Maniac has moved forward, toward his goal; backward, away from his goal; or whether no action concerning his goal was taken. Put a check mark in the corresponding column. Keep in mind how Maniac feels about each place where he lives—does he feel he has found a real home?

Science

Maniac Magee wonders a lot about skin color while he's in Two Mills. What *does* make a person's skin a certain color? Research skin pigmentation. Then write a short essay explaining why skin comes in different colors, including information on melanin.

Social Studies

The racial tensions described in this story were common in America during the 1950s and 1960s. During that time, many people participated in the civil rights movement, working to create racial equality. Learn more about this era by preparing a civil rights dictionary. Research the civil rights movement. On each of ten index cards, write a word relevant to the civil rights movement found in your research. Add a short definition for each word, and then illustrate each definition. Tape the cards end to end and fold accordion-style to make your dictionary.

Language Arts

Choose ten difficult words from the story. Write one of the words in large cursive letters. Below it, write a definition of the word and copy the sentence in which the word is found. Trace the vocabulary word you wrote with glue. Then, beginning with one end of a ball of string, glue the string to the word. When you come to the end of the word, do not cut the string. Allow the glue to dry. Using the same string, continue in the same manner with the next word on another sheet of paper. At the end of the last word, cut the string. You now have one long untangled "Cobble's Knot" of vocabulary words.

Language Arts

The story of Maniac Magee is the making of a legend in Two Mills. But what makes a legend? Obtain a copy of page 21 from your teacher. Follow the directions to identify the elements of a legend in Maniac's story.

Writing

Maniac Magee had a newsworthy first day in Two Mills! On a 10" x 14" sheet of white drawing paper, design a front page for a newspaper titled "The Two Mills Gazette." Choose three or four events from that first day on which to report. Decide which one you think is the most important and make it your lead story. Write articles for each event, including interviews with those involved. Include drawings to represent photographs of the most important news scenes.

There's No Place Like Home

Maniac is in search of a home. Each space below represents one of the places he lives during the story. In each home shape, write about two incidents that happen to Maniac while he lives in that home.

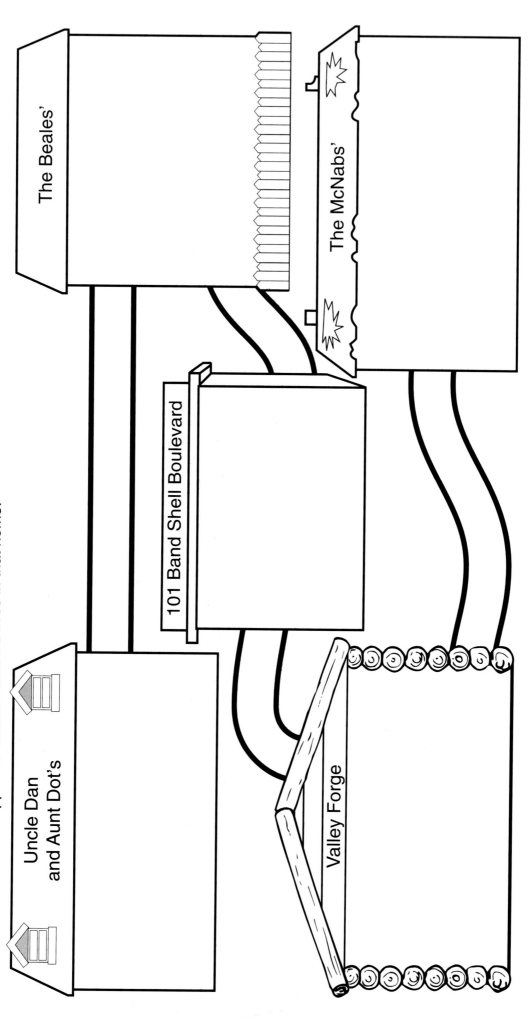

The Beales'

The McNabs'

101 Band Shell Boulevard

Uncle Dan and Aunt Dot's

Valley Forge

Which place finally becomes home to Maniac? Write a paragraph explaining your conclusion on the back of this page.

©2001 The Education Center, Inc. • *Contracts for Independent Readers* • *Realistic Fiction* • TEC789 • Key p. 62

Note to the teacher: Use with activity #1 on page 18.

The Legend of Maniac Magee

Maniac Magee was a legend in Two Mills, but is his story really a legend? Each box below is labeled with one of the elements that makes a story a legend. Examine Maniac's story for the elements of a legend. In each box, write two incidents from the book that are examples of the corresponding element. On the back of this page, write a paragraph explaining why you think the story of Maniac Magee is or is not a legend.

1. A legend is set in a non-specific historical past.

2. A legend doesn't have just one source.

3. A legend starts by being told orally, with different versions.

4. Characters in a legend are often either all good or all bad.

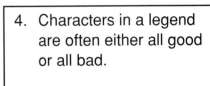

5. Parts of a legend could not or did not really happen in real life.

6. Usually a legend has a lesson or moral to teach.

Sun & Spoon
by Kevin Henkes

About the Book

Two months after Spoon Gilmore's beloved grandmother has died, he realizes that he needs something that has been important to her to remember her by. While visiting his grandfather, he rummages around the house, looking for just the right thing. In the dining room, he sees the suns his grandmother has collected from all over the world. But somehow taking one of Gram's suns just doesn't seem right. Then Spoon remembers the many double solitaire games he has played with Gram and Pa. He remembers Gram's special deck of cards decorated with suns. Since she would have been the last person to touch them, he decides they are the perfect remembrance. But when Spoon takes the cards without asking his grandfather, he unknowingly takes the one thing that Pa is also counting on to help stay close to Gram.

About the Author

Kevin Henkes's writing has the kind of warmth that makes a reader feel snug, as if wrapped in a comforter in front of a crackling fire. Though problems may occur—as they do in real life—his characters deal with them in an atmosphere of comfort and safety.

Henkes was born in Racine, Wisconsin, in November 1960 and grew up in the kind of home that his characters often inhabit. He started drawing as a child and was encouraged by his parents and teachers, but his older brother was considered the real artist of the family. Nevertheless, at 19, Henkes put together a portfolio and spent his life savings on a trip to New York, hoping to find a publisher. On his second day there, he received a contract from Greenwillow Books.

At the time, Henkes thought of himself as an artist, and his first books were picture books, like *Chrysanthemum, Lilly's Purple Plastic Purse,* and *Julius, the Baby of the World.* Henkes claims that he's now beginning to like writing more. His quiet, family-centered novels are as warm and wonderful as his spunky picture book characters. Henkes lives in Madison, Wisconsin, with his wife, Laura, and son Will.

Student Contract Materials List

- Activity #1: paper, pencil
- Activity #2: various art supplies, 12" length of ribbon, 3 small index cards, glue
- Activity #3: reference materials on thunderstorms, ½ sheet of poster board, crayons or markers
- Activity #4: paper, pencil
- Activity #5: reference materials on Madison, Wisconsin; 1 sheet of white construction paper; crayons or markers
- Activity #6: copy of page 25
- Activity #7: dictionary
- Activity #8: gardening guide for your area, 12" x 18" sheet of light-colored construction paper, crayons or markers
- Activity #9: paper, pencil
- Activity #10: pictorial guide to flowers; 12" x 18" sheet of construction paper; crayons, markers, or colored pencils
- Activity #11: reference materials on tattoos
- Activity #12: copy of page 26, orange highlighter, crayons

Sun & Spoon
Independent Contract

Name:_____ Number of activities to be completed: _____

 1. Writing

To make sure that he remembers all of the special things about his grandmother, Spoon makes a list of 52 memories of her. Number a sheet of paper from 1 to 52. Choose a person who means a lot to you and write 52 memories about that person. When you've completed your list, give the person a copy to show how special he or she is to you.

 2. Art

Spoon's grandmother collected suns from all over the world. She had suns made of wood, clay, plaster, metal, and stained glass. Create a sun out of your choice of art supplies. Glue a 12-inch ribbon to the bottom of the sun. On each of three small index cards, write one special thing Spoon remembers about his grandmother. Glue the cards about an inch apart on the ribbon.

 3. Science

A huge rainstorm blows through Spoon's neighborhood, leaving behind broken branches in his yard and puddles of water in Pa's house. Research thunderstorms and use the information you find to create a storm timeline. On your timeline, illustrate and describe each stage of a storm in chronological order.

 4. Writing

Spoon's little sister Joanie keeps a suitcase filled with sticks that mean something special to her, but no one knows what they mean. Joanie calls her sticks "bones." Spoon wonders what the bones really mean to Joanie. Pretend you are Joanie. Write a journal entry explaining why you collect "bones" and what the bones mean to you.

 5. Research

The book *Sun & Spoon* takes place in Madison, Wisconsin. Research Madison, Wisconsin. Fold a sheet of white construction paper in thirds to create a brochure. Label the front of the brochure "Madison, Wisconsin" and illustrate it with a picture of the city. Inside the brochure, write information describing the city, including sections on demographics (such as population), recreation, and natural resources. Illustrate each section. On the back of the brochure, write a slogan for Madison that would make tourists want to visit the city.

 6. Writing

Sun & Spoon has four main parts: The Search, The Sun, The Storm, and The Sign. Obtain a copy of page 25 from your teacher. Follow the directions to brainstorm ideas for your own four-part story. Then write your story on the back of the page. Use additional sheets of paper as needed.

Sun & Spoon

Independent Contract

Name:_____ Number of activities to be completed: _____

 Critical Thinking

When Spoon takes his grandmother's solitaire cards without asking, he finds himself caught in an ethical dilemma. Using a dictionary, look up the meaning of the words *ethics, ethical,* and *dilemma.* Copy the definitions and use them to help you write a definition of the term *ethical dilemma.* Reread chapters 10–12. Then write a short essay explaining why you think Spoon's decision about whether to return the cards was an ethical dilemma.

 Science

Spoon's parents often work in their garden, where they grow flowers and vegetables. Consult a gardening guide showing which flowers or vegetables grow best where you live. Then design a garden, including plants that thrive in your area. Draw and label each plant. On the back of the sheet, write about what you would need to do to keep your plants healthy.

 Social Studies

Throughout the book, Spoon is irritated by his little sister Joanie. He doesn't always treat her with kindness. Look back through the book to find three instances where Spoon could have been a better big brother to her. Write what Spoon did; then write what you think he could have done to be a better big brother.

 Language Arts

In chapter 2, Joanie describes the delphiniums in her parents' garden as "teensy blue stars, stuck on a pole." This kind of description is called a *metaphor.* Writers use metaphors to paint word pictures in the reader's mind. Look up the definition of *metaphor.* Then choose ten flowers from a pictorial flower guide. Draw ten squares on a sheet of construction paper. Write the name of each flower at the top of a different square. Draw and color a picture of each flower in the corresponding square; then write a metaphor beneath the picture to describe the flower.

 Research

In chapter 2, Spoon describes the small tattoos his parents have on their hands. Tattooing is an ancient form of body decoration used in many cultures. Research tattoos and then write an article on the history of tattoos. Include information explaining what tattoos have been used for in different cultures. Share your article with the class.

 Social Studies

Spoon and his family plan to travel from their home in Madison, Wisconsin, to his grandmother Evie's home in Eugene, Oregon. Obtain a copy of page 26 from your teacher and discover the shortest and fastest routes from Madison to Eugene.

Make the Connection!

Sun & Spoon has four main parts. Use the book as a model to write your own four-part story. Think about a story with four connecting parts. Use the organizer below to brainstorm each part of your story. Make sure that each idea is connected to the next idea, as in *Sun & Spoon*. Then write your story on the back of this page. Use additional sheets of paper as needed.

The Storm

The Sun

The Sign

The Search

Note to the teacher: Use with activity #6 on page 23.

Road Trip!

The Gilmore family plans to travel from Madison, Wisconsin, to Eugene, Oregon. Follow the directions below to help the Gilmores choose the best route for their road trip.

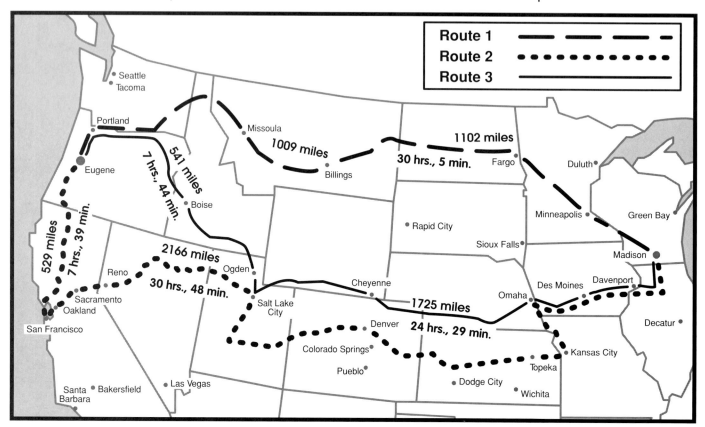

Directions:

1. Label each state on the map.
2. Lightly color Wisconsin yellow and Oregon blue.
3. Highlight Madison and Eugene in orange.
4. For each route, fill in the blanks in the chart to the right.
5. Determine which route is the shortest and which is the fastest. Fill in the corresponding blanks.
6. If the Gilmore family wants to visit the greatest number of states on their trip, which route should they take?_____
7. If they want to visit the fewest states, which route should they take?_____
8. Which route would you take and why?_____

_____

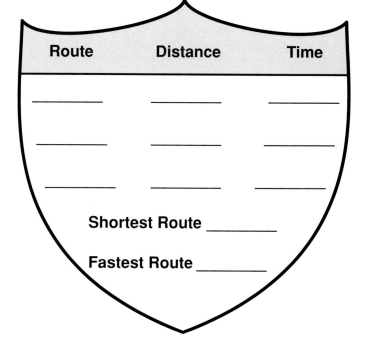

Route	Distance	Time
_____	_____	_____
_____	_____	_____
_____	_____	_____

Shortest Route _____

Fastest Route _____

©2001 The Education Center, Inc. • *Contracts for Independent Readers • Realistic Fiction* • TEC789 • Key p. 62

26   **Note to the teacher:** Use with activity #12 on page 24.

Shiloh
by Phyllis Reynolds Naylor

About the Book

Eleven-year-old Marty Preston discovers a young beagle that has been mistreated. When the dog follows him home, a bond is created between them that will change their lives forever. Although Marty's dad forces him to return the dog to Judd Travers, the dog's cruel owner, Marty silently names the dog Shiloh and vows to save him someday. It's not long before Shiloh runs away from Judd again and returns to Marty. Marty instantly decides that he is not going to let Judd have him back. Marty's plan to keep Shiloh proves difficult, and there are questions of safety, honesty, and responsibility that weigh heavily on the heart of this eleven-year-old boy.

About the Author

Phyllis Reynolds Naylor was born on January 4, 1933, in Anderson, Indiana. Growing up, she lived in Indiana and Illinois. Before Phyllis could write words, she made up stories. She wrote her first book in kindergarten, but it wasn't until many years later, in 1960, that she decided to become a full-time writer. Naylor feels that writing is as natural as breathing. She loves to write and often works on two books at one time.

Naylor writes about things that happen to her, that she reads about, and that she imagines. She clips information from things she reads that are related to an idea she has for a book. She puts these clippings, along with photos, notes, maps, etc., into three-ring notebooks labeled with each book idea. These items help her write her books. The idea for *Shiloh,* the 1992 Newbery Medal winner, came from an abused dog adopted by friends in West Virginia.

Naylor lives in Bethesda, Maryland, with her husband, Rex. They have two sons and two granddaughters. Naylor has authored more than 100 books for children and adults.

Student Contract Materials List

- Activity #1: map of West Virginia, white drawing paper, ruler
- Activity #2: reference materials on beagles, ½ sheet of poster board, crayons or markers
- Activity #3: 2 sheets of different-colored construction paper, glue, scissors, hole puncher, string
- Activity #4: copy of page 30
- Activity #5: telephone book, 12" x 18" light-colored construction paper, crayons or markers

- Activity #6: reference materials on ticks, white drawing paper, crayons or markers
- Activity #7: reference materials on minimum wage
- Activity #8: copy of page 31
- Activity #9: access to the Internet or letter-writing supplies, construction paper, crayons or markers
- Activity #10: copy of page 32
- Activity #11: cardboard, building supplies
- Activity #12: construction paper, crayons or markers

Shiloh

Independent Contract

Name:_____ Number of activities to be completed: _____

1. Social Studies

In chapter 1, Marty describes where he lives. Find the places he mentions on a map of West Virginia. If some places aren't listed on the map, decide where they are based on Marty's description. Then create your own map of the area. Include a scale, a compass rose, and any important landforms, such as rivers and mountains.

2. Research

In the story, we learn about Marty's relationship with Shiloh, but we don't learn much about the characteristics of beagles. Are they really good hunting dogs? Do they make good pets? Research beagles. Then draw a diagram of a beagle, labeling the parts of the dog's body that make it unique. Surround your diagram with at least ten doggie details.

3. Social Studies

Marty makes some comparisons between his friend David and himself. Reread chapter 7 to find the comparisons Marty makes. Then glue two different-colored sheets of construction paper together. Cut a rectangle shape from the glued paper. Write "Marty" on one side and "David" on the other side. For each comparison, cut out a shape from the glued paper. Write about Marty on the side that is the same color as the rectangle labeled "Marty." Write about David in comparison to Marty on the other side. Hole-punch each shape and use string to attach the cutouts to the rectangle shape to create a comparison mobile.

4. Language Arts

Who said that? Can you tell who said something just by reading what was said? Obtain a copy of page 30 from your teacher and try your luck at identifying the speaker of the quotes listed.

5. Science

Write, call, or visit your local humane society to learn more about the proper treatment of pets. Study the information you receive and create a poster titled "The Responsible Pet Owner's List of Top Ten Things to Do for Your Pet." Add illustrations, showing an example of each item on the list. Share your poster with the class.

6. Science

In chapter 2, Marty discovers that Shiloh has ticks. What are ticks? Should Marty be worried? Later, in chapter 12, Marty's dad removes Shiloh's ticks. Did he use the correct procedure? Research ticks. Then create a flyer that shows facts about different types of ticks, why they can be a health threat, and how to keep people and animals safe from them.

©2001 The Education Center, Inc. · *Contracts for Independent Readers · Realistic Fiction* · TEC789

Shiloh

Independent Contract

Name:_____ Number of activities to be completed: _____

7. Math

In the book, Marty works for Judd for $2.00 an hour to earn the $40.00 Judd wants for Shiloh. This is far less than the minimum wage in the United States. How much faster would Marty have been able to buy Shiloh if he had earned minimum wage? Answer this question by finding out what the minimum wage is in your state. Then create two math problems, the first showing how many hours he would have to work at minimum wage and the other at $2.00 an hour. Explain your findings to your class.

8. Critical Thinking

How does Marty's first lie lead to another? What consequences do his lies have? Obtain a copy of page 31 from your teacher to unravel the chain of lies.

9. Social Studies

Was Marty right when he accused Judd of hunting deer out of season? Find out exactly what the hunting laws are in West Virginia by logging onto the Internet and going to www.wvweb.com/www/hunting (current as of August 2000) or writing to the West Virginia Division of Natural Resources, Capitol Complex, Building 3, 1900 Kanawha Boulevard, Charleston, WV 25305. Use the information you find to help you create a Hunter's Handbook. Feature facts and illustrations about the types of animals that can be hunted, hunting season dates, and any other details that would benefit hunters.

10. Language Arts

Several incidents occur in this book that may cause you to feel strong emotions. You may even have your own opinions about whether or not someone in the book made the best choice. Obtain a copy of page 32 from your teacher and take on the role of an expert adviser as you give your opinions about some of the incidents in the book.

11. Art

Now that Shiloh has a permanent home, he'll need a doghouse or shelter. Using cardboard or wood and other building supplies, build a model of a home for Shiloh that Marty would be proud of. Keep Shiloh's size, comfort, and safety in mind as you build.

12. Language Arts

In chapter 15, Marty's dad says, "there's food for the body and food for the spirit. And Shiloh sure enough feeds our spirit." Consider what these words mean. What kind of things feed the spirit? Consider the people, animals, and activities in your life that feed your spirit or make you happy. Create a "Food for the Spirit" menu. Instead of foods you eat, feature things that lift your spirit or make you happy. For example, one item on the menu could be "Dog—A single lick from a dog will keep your face happy for at least a week."

Name _____

Shiloh

🐾 Who Said That? 🐾

Do you know who said each of the quotes below? Test yourself and then check the book to find out how many you answered correctly.

Directions: Read each quote below. In the space provided, write the name of the person who said it. Then look in the book to find out whether you are correct. Record the page number where you find each quote. Give yourself a point for each correctly identified quote. Then tally your score and record it at the bottom to discover your *Shiloh* level. Good luck!

Quote	Person Who Said It	Page Number	Points
1. "It's his concern, Marty, not yours. It's not your dog."			
2. "I want to be a traveling vet."			
3. "If this dog's mistreated, he's only about one out of fifty thousand animals that is."			
4. "Don't you ever, never, aim your gun toward this house or yard."			
5. "Ain't looking for a meal, Mrs. Preston, I'm looking for a dog."			
6. "Even snakes got the right to live."			
7. "You can't just go on electing people to government because they were friends of your father or grandfather."			
8. "So we've got ourselves a secret."			
9. "Marty, don't you *ever* run away from a problem."			
10. "Judd *Travers's?* This the dog he's missing?"			
11. "You've got to go by the law. The law says a man that pays money for a dog owns that dog."			
12. "It wasn't like you *stole* him. That dog come up here on its own."			
13. "He killed one of his dogs in there?"			
14. "I'll pay you two dollars an hour, and that comes to twenty hours to earn forty dollars."			
15. "So we got ourselves a new member of the family."			
16. "You got yourself a dog."			

Total: _____

🐾 16 Points = *Shiloh* Expert   🐾 10 Points = *Shiloh* Novice   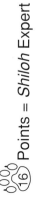 🐾 5 Points = *Shiloh* Apprentice

©2001 The Education Center, Inc. • *Contracts for Independent Readers* • *Realistic Fiction* • TEC789 • Key p. 63

Note to the teacher: Use with activity #4 on page 28.

Chain of Lies

Think about the lies Marty told in order to keep Shiloh a secret. How did one lie cause a chain reaction? Follow the directions below to link the chain of events together.

Directions: Read the situations in the first link in each chain. Decide what lie is told to handle each situation. Write the lie in the second link. In the remaining links, list the events that resulted from the lie. The first one is done for you.

Marty's dad wonders if he's getting too thin, and his mom wonders if she frowns too much.

People start leaving food in their mailboxes for Marty's dad and asking his mom if she's feeling okay.

Mr. Wallace thinks the Prestons need help.

Marty lets Mr. Wallace believe that the old food he is buying is for his family.

Marty needs more food for Shiloh.

Dara Lynn wants to go up and see what Marty is doing on the hill.

Marty's parents want David to come over to spend the day with Marty.

"I also know that you can lie not only by what you say but what you don't say." —Marty

Marty's mom finds out about Shiloh.

Have you ever told a lie that caused a chain of events to occur? On the back of this sheet, make your own chain, including the situation that caused you to lie, the lie, and the events that resulted from your lie. In the final link of your chain, tell how you resolved the situation. Did you tell the truth?

Note to the teacher: Use with activity #8 on page 29.

Dear Expert

Do you want to help others? Do you want to give advice to people in need? The local paper's Expert Adviser gets too many letters to answer them all. Follow the directions below to help the Expert get the job done.

Directions: Read each letter below. Think about what you would do in each person's situation. On the back of this sheet, answer each letter. Begin each letter with "Dear" and the person's assumed name. Then give the letter writer an answer and sign it "Yours truly, The Expert."

Dear Expert,
My son has taken a liking to a dog because he thinks the dog has been mistreated. I told him that since the dog does not belong to us, it's no business of ours how the owner treats it. Did I tell my son the right thing?

Signed, Dad in Distress

Dear Expert,
My brother thinks that little kids can't keep secrets. What do you think?

Sincerely, Secret-Keeping Sister

Dear Expert,
My dad says I should mind my own business about things. He says that what a person does is his own business. I am thinking that there are times when what one person does is everybody's business—like when an animal or a child is mistreated. What do you think, Expert? Should people always mind their own business?

Sincerely, Caring Kid

Dear Expert,
I am very worried. I kept a secret from my husband to help my son. I have never kept a secret from my husband before. I am afraid that if he finds out he will worry that I have kept other things from him, even though I haven't. Should I tell my husband even though I promised my son I wouldn't?

Sincerely, Worried Wife

Dear Expert,
Yesterday, I heard a young man talking back to a neighbor of mine. Can you believe that? It seems like kids just don't respect their elders the way they used to. What do you think about kids talking back to their elders, Expert?

Sincerely, Nosy Neighbor

Dear Expert,
I recently took care of a wounded dog without telling the owner. Now I am worried that the owner could make trouble for me with my patients or damage the reputation I have in town. What should I do?

Sincerely, Doubtful Doc

The Summer of the Swans
by Betsy Byars

About the Book

It's summertime, and 14-year-old Sara is troubled and discontented. She feels like a nobody. She feels that she is not cute, not smart, not a good dancer, and not popular. Her father seems remote, her Aunt Willie is bossy, and her older sister is beautiful. Things are unexpectedly put into perspective for Sara when she awakens one morning to find her mentally retarded younger brother missing. Charlie has wandered off and no one knows where he is. Sara remembers Charlie's love for the swans at the lake and goes to look for him there. As Sara's search grows more desperate, she learns some of life's important lessons and her world comes back into focus.

About the Author

Betsy Byars was born in 1928 in Charlotte, North Carolina. Reading was her favorite subject in school. While growing up, she wanted to work with zoo animals or be a mathematician. However, she majored in English at Queens College. She wrote for *The Saturday Evening Post* and several other magazines.

Byars' first children's book was published in 1962. Since then, she has written more than 50 children's books. It takes Byars about a year to write a novel. She gets writing ideas from events in her life. She  encourages young writers to write about what they know. She believes she's a successful writer because she reads constantly, about a book a day!

The Summer of the Swans won the Newbery Medal in 1971. The story was inspired by a first-grade boy whom Byars tutored. Byars also included something of herself in this novel, as she tries to do in all of her books. When she was little, she had big feet, so she gave big feet to Sara in *The Summer of the Swans*. She currently lives in South Carolina in a house beside an airstrip. The bottom level of her house is a hangar so that she and her husband, Ed—both pilots—can taxi and take off right from home!

Student Contract Materials List

- Activity #1: construction paper, scissors
- Activity #2: drawing paper; colored pencils, markers, or crayons
- Activity #3: dictionary, graph paper
- Activity #4: paper plate, set of watercolors, dictionary
- Activity #5: phone book, large index card
- Activity #6: copy of page 36

- Activity #7: reference materials on swans, one 12" x 18" sheet of light blue construction paper
- Activity #8: drawing paper
- Activity #9: copy of page 37
- Activity #10: ½ sheet of poster board, markers
- Activity #11: copy of page 38
- Activity #12: scraps of construction paper, a twig, twine or raffia, scissors

The Summer of the Swans
Independent Contract

Name:_____ Number of activities to be completed: _____

 1. Writing

Sara is frustrated with her big feet. On a sheet of construction paper, trace around your bare foot. Cut out the shape and write a "footnote" to Sara. In your note, tell Sara what you would like to change about yourself and why. Since Sara can't change the size of her feet, give her some advice on how to deal with her problem.

 2. Art

Early in the book Sara compares herself to Donald Duck because of the big orange tennis shoes she is wearing. While searching for Charlie, Joe compares himself to the cartoon character Wile E. Coyote, "…who is always getting flattened and dynamited and crushed and in the next scene is strolling along, completely normal again." Choose a cartoon or comic strip character with whom you have a trait in common. Draw and color a short comic strip in which the character displays how the two of you are alike.

 3. Social Studies

Various physical land features are mentioned throughout Sara's outdoor adventures. To develop an understanding of the geography of the area in which Sara lives, create a crossword puzzle using the words listed below. Make the geographical definitions of the terms the clues for your puzzle.

pond	ravine	lake
cliff	valley	ditch
bank	forest	

 4. Art

Sara wants to change the color of her shoes from orange to baby blue. But the blue dye turns her orange shoes puce. Complete this color wheel activity to discover some unusual colors. Fold a paper plate in half, in half again, and in half once more. Unfold the plate to reveal eight sections. Along the rim of each section, write one of the following colors: *puce, khaki, chartreuse, taupe, azure, coral, indigo,* and *fuchsia.* Under each word, write the color's dictionary definition. Then mix paint to create each color. Under each definition, paint the section with its corresponding color.

 5. Research

When Aunt Willie realizes that Charlie is missing, she calls the police. If your family had an emergency, would you know what number to call? Have your parent or guardian help you make a list of important emergency numbers on a notecard. Display this card in a prominent location at home for quick reference in case of an emergency.

 6. Reading

Throughout the book, Sara's feelings fluctuate widely. In fact, her feelings toward Joe change drastically from the beginning to the end of the book. Obtain a copy of page 36 from your teacher and take a closer look at Sara's feelings.

The Summer of the Swans

Independent Contract

Name:_____ Number of activities to be completed: _____

 ## Science

Charlie is mesmerized by the swans at the lake. Find out more about swans by researching two of the following swan species: *mute, tundra, whooper, trumpeter, black, black-necked,* and *coscoroba*. Then create a Venn diagram by drawing two overlapping lakes. In each lake, draw and label one of the swans you researched. In the area where the two lakes intersect, list the similarities between the two types of swans. In the lake area around each swan, list how that species differs from the other. Cut out the overlapping lakes along the outer edge. Share your project with the class.

 ## Social Studies

When Sara reaches the top of the hill in her search for Charlie, she is awed by the sight of the valley before her. Reread the beginning of chapter 19. Then draw a map of what Sara sees. Keep in mind that Sara is up high on a mountain and is looking into a valley. Include buildings, forests, and anything else she sees.

 ## Research

The setting for *The Summer of the Swans* is West Virginia. To "climb a mountain" and learn more about West Virginia, obtain a copy of page 37 from your teacher.

 ## Art

At the end of chapter 15, a radio announcer reports that Charlie is missing. He gives a description of Charlie in the hope that someone may have seen him. Using the announcer's description and the description of Charlie in chapter 2, create a missing-child poster of Charlie. Include a drawing of Charlie as well as a written description. Title your poster "Find This Child!"

 ## Reading

In *The Summer of the Swans*, the characters experience various conflicts. Three types of conflicts arise in the story: conflict between a person and another person, conflict between a person and nature, and conflict between a person and his or her thoughts and desires. Through these conflicts, the characters' eyes are opened and they learn more about themselves and each other. Obtain a copy of page 38 from your teacher to further investigate these three types of conflict.

 ## Writing

Throughout the story, there are events that lead to the climax, in which Charlie is found. Draw six leaf shapes on construction paper and cut them out. Write a sentence describing one event on each leaf. Then poke a hole at the top of each leaf and use twine or raffia to tie your leaves to a twig in the sequence in which they occur.

Fluctuating Feelings

Word Bank					
hurt	loving	irritable	fearful	nervous	peaceful
guilty	angry	embarrassed	ashamed	jealous	anxious

Sara experiences many feelings throughout the story. Help Sara sort out her feelings by following the directions below.

Directions: Read each statement below. Write how Sara feels in each box. (Refer to the word bank or choose emotions not listed.) Then write what happens in the story that supports your decision.

1. Sara's feelings toward Charlie at the beginning of the story

_____
_____
_____

4. Sara's feelings toward Joe after she learns the truth about the watch

_____
_____
_____

2. Sara's feelings toward Wanda

_____
_____
_____

5. Sara's feelings toward her dad

_____
_____
_____

3. Sara's feelings toward Joe before she finds out the truth about the watch

_____
_____
_____

6. Sara's feelings toward Charlie at the end of the book

_____
_____
_____

Note to the teacher: Use with activity #6 on page 34.

Fact-Finding Climb

As Sara searches for Charlie, she climbs the rugged terrain of West Virginia. Learn more about Sara's home state by scaling the mountain of facts below.

Directions: Starting at the base of the mountain, read each statement. Use reference materials on West Virginia to help you fill in the missing words. Then write each numbered letter on the matching flag to reveal the West Virginia state motto. Translated, the motto means "Mountaineers are always free."

$$\overline{\underset{1}{}}\ \overline{\underset{2}{}}\ \overline{\underset{3}{}}\ \overline{\underset{4}{}}\ \overline{\underset{5}{}}\ \overline{\underset{6}{}}\ \overline{\underset{7}{}}$$

$$\overline{\underset{8}{}}\ \overline{\underset{9}{}}\ \overline{\underset{10}{}}\ \overline{\underset{11}{}}\ \overline{\underset{12}{}}\ \overline{\underset{13}{}}$$

$$\overline{\underset{14}{}}\ \overline{\underset{15}{}}\ \overline{\underset{16}{}}\ \overline{\underset{17}{}}\ \overline{\underset{18}{}}\ \overline{\underset{19}{}}$$

8. The western border of West Virginia is formed by the __ __ __ __ / __ __ __ __ __ .
   (with numbers 7 and 15)

7. __ __ __ __ __ __ __ cover 80 percent, or four-fifths, of West Virginia's land area.
   (with numbers 13 and 4)

6. West Virginia is one of our nation's leading producers of __ __ __ __ .
   (with number 5)

5. The capital of West Virginia is __ __ __ __ __ __ __ __ __ __ .
   (with numbers 18, 9, 2)

4. West Virginia's nickname is the __ __ __ __ __ __ __ __ State.
   (with numbers 10, 6)

3. The __ __ __ __ __ __ __ __ __ __ __ is West Virginia's state tree.
   (with numbers 8, 1, 11)

2. The __ __ __ __ __ __ __ __ __ Mountains are located along the eastern border of the Appalachian Ridge and Valley Region.
   (with numbers 16, 19, 12)

1. Across the eastern border of the state are the __ __ __ __ __ __ __ __ __ Moun-tains, which are part of the Appalachian Mountain system.
   (with numbers 14, 17, 3)

Caught in Conflict

In *The Summer of the Swans,* the characters experience various conflicts. Follow the directions below to determine what the characters learn about themselves as a result of the conflicts.
Directions: In each box below, a type of conflict is given. Determine a conflict in the book that matches each type and answer the questions.

1. An example of a **person versus person** conflict happens between _____ and _____ .

What is the conflict? _____

_____

How is the conflict resolved? _____

_____

What lesson is learned? _____

_____

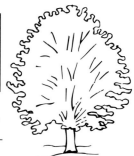

2. An example of a **person versus nature** conflict happens between _____ and _____ .

What is the conflict? _____

_____

How is the conflict resolved? _____

_____

What lesson is learned? _____

_____

3. An example of a **person versus his or her thoughts and desires** conflict happens between _____ and _____ .

What is the conflict? _____

_____

How is the conflict resolved? _____

_____

What lesson is learned? _____

_____

The View From Saturday
by E. L. Konigsburg

About the Book

Four sixth graders are headed toward the state middle school Academic Bowl championship. At first glance, these four sixth graders appear to have nothing in common, but they are destined to become a group called The Souls. Each of them has his or her own story to tell. So does their teacher, Mrs. Olinski, who wonders just how she's come to pick this unlikely foursome to become members of the Academic Bowl team and, even more surprisingly, how they have all come to share such a deep connection. Could something as simple as Saturday afternoon tea have anything to do with it? Somehow, perhaps through a twist of fate, The Souls and their teacher discover how their individual journeys have been woven together with common threads, the threads of friendship and kindness.

About the Author

Elaine Loble Konigsburg was born in New York, New York, in 1930, but grew up in small towns in Pennsylvania. In college she majored in chemistry. Upon graduating, she married David Konigsburg and moved to Florida, where she taught chemistry at a private girls' school until the first of her three children was born. While her children were young, she stayed at home with them. It wasn't until her youngest child went to school that she began her writing career. Konigsburg enjoys not only writing but painting as well. She has illustrated several books.

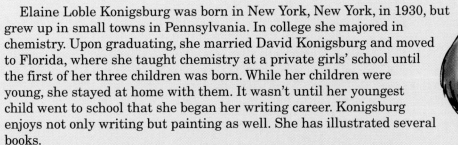

Konigsburg remembers the morning she was walking along the beach and recalled several short stories in her files that were united by a single theme. She used these stories as her inspiration for writing *The View From Saturday*. With this book, Konigsburg began her journey toward winning the Newbery Medal for the second time in her career.

Student Contract Materials List

- **Activity #1:** 2 plant seeds, 2 plastic cups, potting soil, water, tea bags
- **Activity #2:** reference materials on Florida sea turtles, shoebox, crayons or markers, craft supplies, scissors, glue
- **Activity #3:** copy of page 42
- **Activity #4:** blank videotape, video camera, VCR, TV
- **Activity #5:** paper, pencil
- **Activity #6:** white drawing paper, crayons or markers

- **Activity #7:** reference materials on tea, light-colored construction paper, crayons or markers
- **Activity #8:** several issues of a local newspaper
- **Activity #9:** cookbooks, access to the grocery store
- **Activity #10:** copy of page 43
- **Activity #11:** crayons or markers
- **Activity #12:** ½ sheet of poster board, crayons or markers, scissors

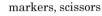

The View From Saturday

Independent Contract

Name:_____   Number of activities to be completed: _____

1. Science

The Souls meet on Saturdays to drink tea. What else can be done with tea? Find out whether tea can improve the growth of a plant by conducting an experiment. Plant two seeds in two separate plastic cups. Water one plant with regular tap water and the second plant with tea that is made using a tea bag. What do you think will happen? Use the scientific method to conduct your experiment and then report your findings to the class.

2. Science

In chapter 2, Nadia tells about writing a report on the five different types of Florida sea turtles: loggerheads, greens, leatherbacks, hawksbills, and Kemp's ridleys. Select one of the five types of turtles. Research this turtle and its habitat. Then construct a shoebox diorama showing the turtle in its habitat. Write a brief paragraph detailing the main features of the turtle's habitat; then cut it out and glue it to the back of your diorama.

3. Language Arts

In chapter 2, Nadia mentions how her life has changed since her parents' divorce. Obtain a copy of page 42 from your teacher to compare her former life with her present life.

4. Language Arts

In chapter 9, Holly Blackwell, anchorwoman for Channel Three Eyewitness News, visits with The Souls but unfortunately asks Mrs. Olinski only one question and asks The Souls nothing. Imagine that you are a famous anchorperson and you are going to interview Mrs. Olinski or one of The Souls. Make a list of at least ten questions. Then ask a friend who has read the book to be one of the characters while you conduct the interview. Videotape the interview and then play it for your class.

5. Reading

There are 12 chapters in this book, none of which have a title. However, several chapters have smaller sections, some of which are titled—for example, "Noah Writes a B & B Letter" and "Nadia Tells of Turtle Love." Take on the role of a book editor by writing a title for each chapter and then making a table of contents. Be sure to include the following information for each chapter in your table of contents: chapter number, chapter title, and page numbers.

6. Social Studies

The Souls learn about friendship and kindness at their Saturday afternoon teas. Brainstorm a list of kind acts that you could perform for the special people in your life. For example, you could wash the dishes, sharpen the class pencils, or help a friend with a homework assignment. Use your list to create a colorful ten-page Kindness Coupon Booklet. On each coupon write the recipient's name, the act of kindness you will perform, when you will perform the act, and your signature. Give your coupons as gifts on special occasions or for no reason at all—just as an act of kindness!

The View From Saturday

Independent Contract

Name:_____   Number of activities to be completed: _____

 7. **Research**

Tea is a very important part of the story told in *The View From Saturday*. Besides drinking tea, what are some other uses for tea and tea leaves? Research tea and tea leaves to find other uses for them. Then create a booklet shaped like a tea leaf and fill it with tea facts and illustrations.

 8. **Social Studies**

In chapter 7, Mr. Homer Fairbain, the master of ceremonies for the district playoffs, has had five letters to the editor published about him in the newspaper, none of them favorable. Look through several issues of your local newspaper and read the letters to the editor. Pick a topic of interest in your community, one that you feel strongly about, and write a letter to the editor expressing your opinion on the topic. Send your letter to the newspaper office. Then check your newspaper on a regular basis—maybe your letter will be selected for publication!

 9. **Math**

At his tea party, Julian serves small sandwiches and pastries. Find a recipe that could be used to make a tea party treat like Julian's. Copy the ingredients for making the treat. Visit a grocery store to locate the needed ingredients. Write down the name of each ingredient, along with its price and size. Calculate the total cost of the ingredients. Then figure out how much it will cost to make your recipe. Based on the number of servings your recipe makes, what would the cost be for one serving? Share this information with your class and explain how you have determined the cost of each serving.

 10. **Critical Thinking**

A TV producer has called on you to help turn *The View From Saturday* into a movie. Your assignment is to cast people for the roles in the upcoming film. Obtain a copy of page 43 from your teacher and then start casting!

 11. **Writing**

Consider how the story would be different if you were the fourth and final member of The Souls, not Julian. Make a list of what would be different. Use your list to write a new ending for the outcome of the Academic Bowl. Illustrate this new ending, putting yourself in Julian's place.

 12. **Art**

E. L. Konigsburg uses different characters to tell different parts of the story. She also skips back and forth between the present and the past. The story can be compared to a puzzle; you have to put all of the little pieces together before you can see the big picture. Create your own story puzzle. First, make a poster that includes information on the characters, setting, and plot. Then draw pictures to go along with the information. Next, draw puzzle piece shapes on the back and cut them out. Finally, challenge a friend who has read the book to put it back together.

Nadia's Life Has Changed

When Nadia's parents get a divorce, Nadia experiences many changes. Follow the directions below to sort out how her life changes and how it stays the same.

Part I Directions: Complete the Venn diagram below by filling in the left side with details about how Nadia's life was before the divorce. Fill in the right side with details about how her life is different after the divorce. In the center, list things that have stayed the same. If needed, reread "Nadia Tells of Turtle Love."

Nadia's Life Before
the Divorce

Things
That Have
Stayed the Same

Nadia's Life After
the Divorce

Part II Directions: Think about an event that has changed your life. On the back of this sheet, draw a Venn diagram comparing how your life was before this event and how it has been different since the event. In the middle, list the things that have stayed the same.

©2001 The Education Center, Inc. • *Contracts for Independent Readers* • *Realistic Fiction* • TEC789 • Key p. 63

42 **Note to the teacher:** Use with activity #3 on page 40.

Lights, Camera, Action!

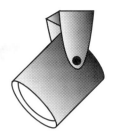

A TV producer has called on you to help with casting the upcoming movie based on *The View From Saturday.* You can choose famous actors, friends, relatives, or classmates. Follow the directions below to begin your movie-casting career!

Directions: Read the list of roles below. Next to each role, write the name of the person you are casting in that role and the reason you think that person is the best choice for the part.

Role	Person Cast	Person's Qualifications
Noah Gershom		
Nadia Diamondstein		
Ethan Potter		
Julian Singh		
Mrs. Eva Marie Olinski		
Mr. Singh		
Izzy Diamondstein		
Margaret Draper		
Hamilton Knapp		
Dr. Roy Clayton Rohmer		
Mr. Homer Fairbain		
Ginger		

Which role would you be best suited for? Which role would you most want to play? Are your answers the same? Explain. _____

_____

_____

Walk Two Moons

by Sharon Creech

About the Book

Salamanca Tree Hiddle is traveling from Ohio to Idaho with her grandparents, hoping desperately to find her mother and bring her back home. Along the way, Sal tells her grandparents about her friend, Phoebe. After Phoebe's mother disappears and several strange messages arrive, Phoebe is convinced that her mother has been kidnapped by a lunatic. Sal just wants things to be the way they were before her own mother left. To bring her mother back home, Sal believes she must get to Idaho by August 20, her mother's birthday. Her father tells her she is just "fishing in the air," but Sal has to see her mother for herself to know that she won't be coming back.

About the Author

Sharon Creech was born in 1945 near Cleveland, Ohio. She grew up in a family of imaginative storytellers. Sharon loved to read Greek and American Indian myths and the legends of King Arthur. She dreamed of becoming a writer who created mysterious, magical worlds for readers to explore. Stories and the tools for writing held a fascination for her. Sharon loved the new pens, pencils, books, and paper she would get at the start of each new school year. Inspired by her teachers, Sharon developed her natural gift for writing and passion for books into a dual career as a teacher and writer.

Creech has traveled throughout Europe and has taught in American schools in England and Switzerland. She currently lives in England nine months of each year. During the summers, Creech visits the United States to spend time with her two grown children.

Creech has published novels for children and adults, as well as poetry and short stories. In 1995, Creech was awarded the Newbery Award for *Walk Two Moons.* It was also named a Notable Book of the Year by the American Library Association.

Student Contract Materials List

- Activity #1:   copy of page 47
- Activity #2:   crayons or markers
- Activity #3:   1 sheet of 8½" x 11" white paper
- Activity #4:   1 sheet of 9" x 12" light-colored construction paper, crayons or markers, reference materials on poisonous snakebites
- Activity #5:   paper, pencil
- Activity #6:   copy of page 48
- Activity #7:   copy of page 49, U.S. atlas

- Activity #8:   one 5" x 8" index card, crayons or markers
- Activity #9:   1 sheet of 12" x 18" light-colored construction paper, crayons or markers
- Activity #10:   1 sheet of 9" x 12" white construction paper, crayons or markers
- Activity #11:   U.S. road map
- Activity #12:   scissors, stapler, crayons or markers

Walk Two Moons
Independent Contract

Name:_____ Number of activities to be completed: _____

 1. ## Reading

"Everyone has his own agenda" is one of the messages left on the Winterbottom's porch. Gram explains the message by saying, "Everybody is just walking along concerned with his own problems, his own life, his own worries." Each of the main characters has an agenda, a set of problems, goals, worries, and hardships. Obtain a copy of page 47 from your teacher and learn about each character's agenda.

 2. ## Writing

Sal's mother deeply appreciated the beauty of nature. Write an *ode,* or a poem that praises a person or thing using dignified language, about something found in nature, such as the sky, a tree, or a river. Write as if you are speaking directly to the thing. Use a thesaurus to help you choose high-sounding words and phrases to praise the thing. Use either rhyming or free verse. Write at least eight lines and capitalize the first word in each line. After editing your work, copy your ode using fancy handwriting. Then add a decorative border with a nature theme.

 3. ## Art

Mr. Birkway has his students draw pictures of their souls. On a piece of white drawing paper, draw a picture of your soul. Try to complete your drawing in 15 seconds (as Mr. Birkway instructed his class). Then write a brief paragraph below your drawing explaining how it accurately represents your soul. Include the meaning of the symbols you used and tell what makes your soul unique.

 4. ## Science

After Gram is bitten by a poisonous snake, Gramps and Tom Fleet (the boy they meet at the river) use first aid procedures to treat the wound. Research proper emergency treatment for poisonous snakebites. Then prepare an emergency first aid pamphlet that gives step-by-step instructions for treating a victim of a poisonous snakebite. Include a diagram for each step.

 5. ## Social Studies

People may respond to their experiences by making positive or negative choices. In *Walk Two Moons,* Sal, Phoebe, Sal's mother, and Mrs. Winterbottom each respond negatively to events in their lives. Fold your paper in half; then fold it in half again. Label each of the four sections with the name of a different character listed above. On each section, describe an event in the character's life and her negative response. Think about positive choices the character could have made instead. Record two of these choices and describe the possible consequences of each.

 6. ## Reading

As Sal struggles to accept her mother's death, she meets other characters who have problems of their own. Eventually, she learns to "walk two moons in their moccasins" and finds that she has thoughts and feelings in common with them. Obtain a copy of page 48 from your teacher. Complete the activity as directed to compare Sal's experiences and emotions with those of other characters.

Walk Two Moons

Independent Contract

Name:_____ Number of activities to be completed: _____

 7.) Social Studies

Sal has "a way with maps," so she can help Gram and Gramps find their way from Euclid, Ohio, to Lewiston, Idaho. Gramps is excited about seeing "the whole ding-dong country," and Gram is looking forward to spending time with Sal. Reread the parts of the story that tell you what happens to the family along the way. Obtain a copy of page 49 from your teacher and put the story events in order.

 8.) Writing

Sal's mother left home because "she needed to learn about what she was." She hoped her cousin would help her find herself. If you wanted to learn more about yourself, where would you go? Which person in your life would you trust to help you? Obtain a 5" x 8" index card and pretend it is a postcard. Draw and color a picture of the place you would go to find the "real you." On the back, write a message home. Explain why you chose this place and what you hope to discover about yourself.

 9.) Social Studies

Walk Two Moons is a story about families—Sal's, Phoebe's, and Ben's. Family members are connected to one another and to others—such as friends, pets, and teachers—in special ways. Create a family tree showing your connections. Draw a tree with branches. Write your name near the top of the trunk. On the branches, add the names of people with whom you feel connections. When you finish, draw a leaf shape around each name. Then color the leaves naming family members of the blood green. Color the leaves naming family members of the heart (friends and pets) yellow.

 10.) Art

The messages left on the Winterbottoms' front porch seem to have mysterious, deeper meanings that Sal and Phoebe have trouble understanding. Reread the messages listed in chapter 29. Create a greeting card for one of the characters in the book using one of the messages. Fold a sheet of construction paper in half to make the card. On the front, write and illustrate the message you chose. Inside the card, write a poem or message to the character that explains the saying's deeper meaning and tells the character what you think the message should mean to her.

 11.) Math

Sal and her grandparents travel from Ohio to Idaho in seven days. Along the way, they visit national parks and other tourist attractions. Obtain a U.S. road map from your teacher. Starting at your hometown, plan a seven-day trip through five states. Identify national parks, historic sites, and other tourist attractions to visit along the way. Using the mileage scale on your road map, calculate the distance between each attraction. Then, using an average speed of 60 miles per hour, estimate the driving time between each stop. Plan a trip itinerary. Calculate the amount of time needed for travel, meals, sleep, and sight-seeing.

 12.) Reading

Sharon Creech uses a literary device known as *foreshadowing*. Foreshadowing gives clues or hints to the reader about later events in the story, which are not fully understood until the end of the book. Review *Walk Two Moons* to find clues that foreshadow what happened to Sal's mother. Make a detective's clue book and use it to record the clues you find. To make the clue book, stack two sheets of notebook paper. Fold them in half horizontally and cut them in half vertically. Stack all four pages and staple along the fold to make an eight-page notebook. Copy the clues you detected and illustrate the book.

Everyone Has an Agenda

Each of the main characters in the book has an agenda. On each scroll, beneath the character's name, write his or her main goal. Then briefly describe the problems, worries, and hardships the character needs to overcome on the way to reaching the goal.

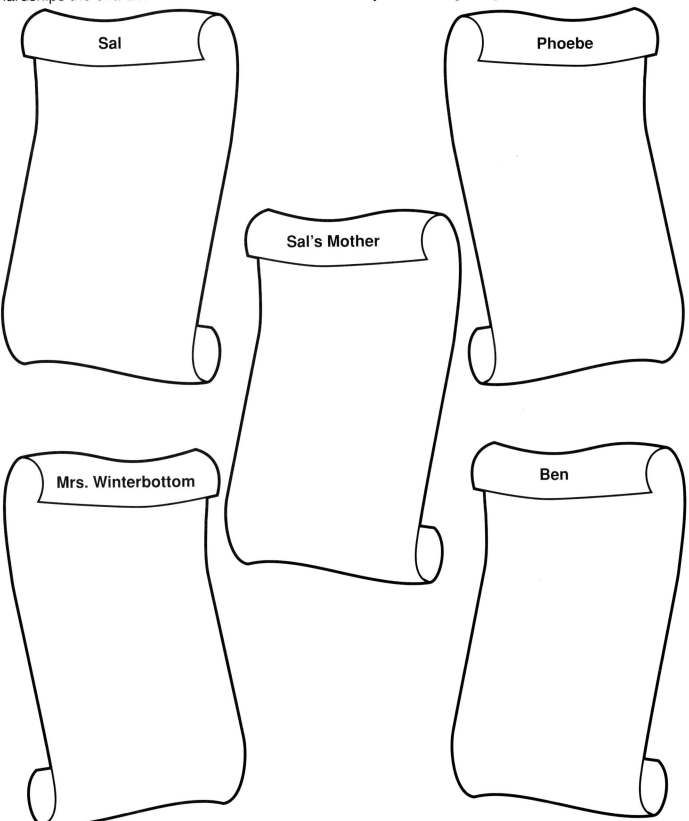

Sal

Phoebe

Sal's Mother

Mrs. Winterbottom

Ben

Walk Two Moons

Other characters in *Walk Two Moons* have feelings and problems like Sal's. Read the information about Sal on the chart below. Then write the name of a character who has a similar problem and tell how it compares with Sal's experience. The first one has been done for you.

Sal	Other Characters
1. Sal's mother went away to find herself.	Phoebe's mother went away to find herself.
2. Sal thinks she can bring her mother back.	
3. Sal needed to go to Idaho to see her mother.	
4. Sal wants to help her father deal with her mother's death.	
5. Sal was unkind to her mother before her mother left.	
6. Sal drew her soul as a circle containing a maple leaf.	
7. Sal feels jealous that her mother wanted another baby.	
8. Sal tries to make up reasons for her mother leaving.	
9. Sal learns to deal with the loss of her mother by doing things her mother did.	
10. Sal doesn't want her father to care about someone other than her mother.	

Note to the teacher: Use with activity #6 on page 45.

Name_____

On the Road to Idaho

As the story ends, Sal realizes that the trip from Euclid, Ohio, to Lewiston, Idaho, is a gift for her from her grandparents. The trip gives Sal a chance to "walk in her mother's moccasins" as she visits the places her mother has been.

Directions: On the line below each box, identify the state in which each incident took place. Then number the moccasins in the order the events happened.

1. While visiting Mount Rushmore, Sal wonders why whoever carved the presidents couldn't have carved a couple of American Indians too.

2. The three travelers smoke a long peace pipe with an American Indian at Pipestone National Monument.

3. Sal visits the site of the bus accident and her mother's grave.

4. The Hiddles stop in the Badlands, where Sal sees jagged peaks, steep gorges, and pink, purple, and black rocks.

5. Sal gets separated from her grandparents and then finds Gram dancing in the center of a group of American Indians.

6. Gram is so excited about seeing Old Faithful that she cries.

7. Sal, Gram, and Gramps go straight to the hospital in Coeur d'Alene.

8. The Hiddles stop at a rest area and Gramps decides to help a woman having car trouble.

9. While swimming in the Missouri River near Chamberlain, Gram is bitten by a water moccasin.

Note to the teacher: Use with activity #7 on page 46.

Yang the Youngest and His Terrible Ear

by Lensey Namioka

About the Book

The Yang family has recently moved from China to the United States. Everyone in the family is musically talented except the youngest child, Yingtao. After years of violin lessons from his father, Yingtao plays terribly. The truth is, Yingtao is tone-deaf, so he cannot hear his mistakes. Soon after arriving in Seattle, Yingtao discovers a natural ability for playing baseball. But Yingtao still has a problem. He is to be in a recital with his brother and sisters. He knows that no matter how much he practices, he will ruin the recital. Yingtao, his sister, and his best friend devise a plan that makes the recital a success and helps the Yangs accept Yingtao's natural gift for playing baseball.

About the Author

Born in Beijing, China, Lensey Namioka grew up in a musical family. She, like Yingtao, had a terrible ear. She coped with her tone deafness by learning to play the oboe, an instrument with fixed pitch.

As an author, Namioka has written books for children and adults. She attended Radcliffe College and earned a master's degree from the University of California, Berkeley. The American Library Association honored Namioka's *Village of the Vampire Cat* and *Island of Ogres* by selecting those books as Best Books of the Year. Namioka has two grown daughters and lives with her husband in Seattle, Washington.

Student Contract Materials List

- Activity #1: copy of page 53
- Activity #2: drawing paper, crayons or markers
- Activity #3: paper, pencil
- Activity #4: reference materials on Asian languages, map of Asia, drawing paper, colored pencils
- Activity #5: different-sized boxes, different-sized rubber bands
- Activity #6: reference materials on Babe Ruth or Isaac Stern, drawing paper, crayons or markers
- Activity #7: copy of page 54
- Activity #8: watercolors, paintbrush, manila paper
- Activity #9: tape player
- Activity #10: copy of page 55
- Activity #11: paper, pencil
- Activity #12: reference materials on Seattle, drawing paper, crayons or markers

Yang the Youngest and His Terrible Ear

Independent Contract

Name:_____   Number of activities to be completed: _____

---

1. Reading

In chapter 3, Yingtao has difficulty understanding English words that have more than one meaning, such as *strike* and *plate*. Obtain a copy of page 53 from your teacher to help Yingtao choose the correct meaning and score a big hit for his team.

2. Art

Lensey Namioka opens her story with language that creates a wonderful picture in our minds. As each of the three elder siblings plays an instrument, Namioka's words paint a picture.
"…a shower of sparkling notes fell over the room."
"…a rainbow of notes hung brightly in the air."
"…a wave of deep, mellow notes washed over us."
Choose one of these descriptive phrases and illustrate its literal meaning.

3. Writing

In chapter 4, Yingtao sees Matthew's room for the first time. Yingtao finds it strange that Matthew displays pictures of major league baseball players and concert violinists on his walls. It is obvious that Matthew admires both baseball players and concert violinists. Make a Venn diagram showing the similarities and differences between a major league baseball player and a concert violinist. Use your Venn diagram to write two paragraphs comparing and contrasting the two professions.

4. Social Studies

When Yingtao registers for school, he writes "Chinese" in the space marked "race." The school secretary tells him to change it to "Asian-American." The secretary goes on to say that there are many Asian-Americans at the school and that he should be able to make friends easily. The secretary makes it sound as if all Asian-Americans are alike. Research to find out how many Asian countries and languages there are. Draw, copy, or trace a map of Asia and use colored pencils to show the areas where different languages are spoken.

5. Science

The violin, the viola, and the cello all look alike except for size. Being different sizes, they produce different sounds. Using different-sized boxes and rubber bands, create two different stringed instruments. Make one instrument to produce very high tones and the other to produce low tones. Write notes about what you discover concerning the sound and size of your instruments.

6. Research

Two professional personalities are mentioned in the book. Babe Ruth is known as the "Sultan of Swat" and was one of baseball's greatest players. Isaac Stern is recognized as one of the world's greatest violinists. Choose one of these two talented individuals to research. Then write a newspaper article highlighting an event in his life as if it just happened. Be sure to add a biographical sketch. Draw a picture of the person to go along with your article.

Yang the Youngest and His Terrible Ear

Independent Contract

Name: _____ Number of activities to be completed: _____

 Reading (7.)

An idiom is an expression that can't be determined by the meanings of its words. For example, "It's raining cats and dogs." This sounds as if cats and dogs are falling from the sky, but the idiom means that it is raining very hard. Idioms add color to a language, but they can make it difficult to learn a language. Obtain a copy of page 54 from your teacher and explore some idioms that may have perplexed Yingtao the first time he heard them.

 Art (8.)

In chapter 5, Yingtao convinces his parents that a decorative screen would make a nice background for the recital. Second Sister immediately starts to paint scenes she remembers from China. She paints one screen of rocky mountains covered with pine trees. In another she paints a boat going down a river. Using watercolors and a sheet of manila paper folded into thirds, paint landscapes of special places you remember.

 Music (9.)

In chapter 3, Yingtao enjoys the lip sync skits put on by the fifth graders. The lip sync is the inspiration for his plan to save the recital. Choose an audiotape of your favorite song and prepare a lip sync. Present your lip sync to the class.

 Math (10.)

The Yang family is originally from Shanghai, China. Perhaps the Yang family would like to return there for vacation one day. Obtain a copy of page 55 from your teacher and use your math skills to find the answers to some travel questions.

 Writing (11.)

Yingtao doesn't have a good ear for music, but he has a good eye for the strike zone. Yingtao is very pleased to find out that he is good at something. Yingtao is so excited that he feels like floating away into the sky. Choose a personal strength that you possess and write a story telling about the time you first discovered that it was a strength of yours.

 Research (12.)

Seattle, Washington, has many wonderful sights. Research Seattle and create a travel brochure advertising the city. Your brochure should include historic sites, tourist attractions, athletic arenas, and other points of interest found in Seattle.

The Ballplayer's Terrible Confusion

The score is 11 to 9 and Yingtao's team is losing. It's the bottom of the ninth inning. The bases are loaded as Yingtao steps up to bat. Follow the directions below to find out if Yingtao helps his team win the game.

Directions: Read each sentence and definition below. Determine the correct meaning for the bold-faced word. Then color the ball with the matching letter to determine the result of each of Yingtao's swings.

1. The batter steps up to the **plate** in hopes of hitting a home run.
   a. a flat dish used to hold food
   b. a five-sided piece of rubber set into the ground

   (a) strike   (b) ball

2. The umpire yells **"Strike!"** as the ball whizzes past.
   a. failed attempt of a batter to hit the ball
   b. to hit something

   (a) strike   (b) ball

3. If the umpire calls a **ball** one more time, the batter will walk to first base.
   a. a pitch that goes outside of the strike zone and is not swung at
   b. a round object used in games and sports

   (a) strike   (b) ball

4. The crowd cheers as the player scores the first **run** of the game.
   a. to enter into an election race
   b. the score a baseball player makes as he crosses home plate

   (a) foul ball   (b) ball

5. The batter keeps his eye on the pitcher and is ready to **swing.**
   a. a seat that freely moves back and forth
   b. a blow made with a sweeping arm movement

   (a) strike   (b) ball

6. The nervous **batter** hopes he will hit the ball out of the ballpark.
   a. a baseball player who is up at bat
   b. a mixture of mainly flour, eggs, and milk or water

   (a) foul ball   (b) home run

7. The team's **uniform** is blue with white trim.
   a. dress of a particular group to serve as identification
   b. having the same form, not varying

   (a) home run   (b) strike

Who won the game and what was the final score? _____

You Know What I Mean?

Directions: Read each idiom below. In the thought bubble, draw a picture of what Yingtao might have imagined when he first heard the expression. Then write the idiom's meaning in the space provided.

1. Chapter 1

I have a terrible ear for music!

Meaning:

2. Chapter 3

What's bugging you?

Meaning:

3. Chapter 4

All eyes are on you!

Meaning:

4. Chapter 5

I really played my heart out.

Meaning:

Note to the teacher: Use with activity #7 on page 52.

Shanghai Vacation

The six members of the Yang family are planning a fabulous Shanghai vacation. Complete the chart and answer the questions below to help the Yangs find the best deal.

1. Read the chart below. Which airline do you think has the cheapest prices? _____

2. Complete the chart by finding the total cost for the Yang family to fly to Shanghai on each airline.

Airline	Adult Ticket Price	Child Ticket Price	Discount	Yang Family Total
In-the-Clouds Airline	$589.00	$589.00	10%	
Over-the-Treetops Airline	$650.00	$575.00	---	
Skyline Flights	$725.00	$695.00	20%	
Through-the-Air Airline	$843.00	$426.00	---	

3. Which airline has the best deal? _____

4. Was your prediction correct? _____

5. Which airline would cost the Yangs the most money? _____

6. What is the price difference between the least expensive airline and the most expensive airline?

    _____

7. If there were no discounts, which airline would have the best deal? _____

    The worst deal? _____

8. If the Over-the-Treetops Airline offered a 5 percent discount, what would be the total price for the Yangs? _____

Yolonda's Genius

by Carol Fenner

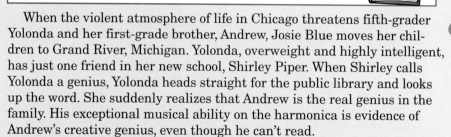

About the Book

When the violent atmosphere of life in Chicago threatens fifth-grader Yolonda and her first-grade brother, Andrew, Josie Blue moves her children to Grand River, Michigan. Yolonda, overweight and highly intelligent, has just one friend in her new school, Shirley Piper. When Shirley calls Yolonda a genius, Yolonda heads straight for the public library and looks up the word. She suddenly realizes that Andrew is the real genius in the family. His exceptional musical ability on the harmonica is evidence of Andrew's creative genius, even though he can't read.

One day, when Yolonda forgets to walk her brother home from school, a gang harasses Andrew and destroys his precious harmonica. Yolonda replaces the instrument but Andrew has stopped making music. Determined to help her brother, Yolonda manages to introduce him to famous musicians at a blues festival, restoring his spirit and calling their mother's attention to Andrew's extraordinary gift.

About the Author

Carol Fenner was born in New York on September 30, 1929. She was the oldest of five children. Her love of words and books was nurtured by her mother who would read poetry at bedtime. Her Aunt Phyllis—a librarian, writer, and delightful storyteller—provided a wealth of children's books for Carol and her siblings.

Even when she was very young, Carol made up poetry. She would come in from playing outside and announce to her mother, "I feel a poem coming on," and her mother would write it down. Carol started out writing poetry and stories. When she was about eleven, she ventured into playwriting and then started writing a novel in her teenage years. Carol also became interested in drawing and has illustrated several of her own books.

Fenner won the American Library Association Notable Book citation for *Tigers in the Cellar* and *Gorilla, Gorilla*. In 1996, Fenner won the Newbery Honor Book award for *Yolonda's Genius*. Other titles by Fenner are *The Skates of Uncle Richard*, *A Summer of Horses*, and *Randall's Wall*.

Student Contract Materials List

- Activity #1: dictionary
- Activity #2: copy of page 59
- Activity #3: 9" x 12" light-colored construction paper, crayons or markers, arts-and-crafts supplies
- Activity #4: classified section of the newspaper showing ads for musical instruments, ruler
- Activity #5: copy of page 60
- Activity #6: five drinking glasses, water, metal spoon
- Activity #7: paper, pencil

- Activity #8: reference materials on classical, jazz, and blues musicians; construction paper; crayons or markers
- Activity #9: jump rope, Internet access
- Activity #10: white drawing paper; crayons, markers, or colored pencils; Internet access
- Activity #11: used magazines or catalogs featuring musical instruments, wire coat hanger, glue, string, scissors, construction paper, crayons or markers
- Activity #12: paper, pencil

Yolonda's Genius

Independent Contract

Name:_____ Number of activities to be completed: _____

1. Language Arts

After Shirley calls her a genius, Yolonda makes a beeline for the reference section of the public library. In the dictionary, she discovers the meaning of the word. Increase your vocabulary by using a dictionary to learn the meaning of unfamiliar words in *Yolonda's Genius*. Fold a piece of paper in half twice in each direction to create 16 squares. Look back through the novel to find 16 unfamiliar words and copy each one on a square. Using a dictionary, look up each word's definition and write it in the square. Then, on the back of the sheet in the corresponding square, write a sentence using each word.

2. Language Arts

Chicago, Illinois, and Grand River, Michigan, are as different as night and day. Obtain a copy of page 59 from your teacher. Follow the directions on the page to compare the two places.

3. Writing

Have you ever tried songwriting? In chapter 10 when Aunt Tiny arrives, Yolonda dashes to the piano to play an original song. Yolonda's song is like a *clerihew,* a humorous four-line rhyming poem based on a person. The person's name is one of the rhymes. A clerihew is a *quatrain,* or four-line poem, with an *aabb* rhyming pattern. Try writing a clerihew about someone who is important to you. Then feature the poem on a greeting card for that person. Frame the clerihew with a decorative border.

4. Math

The cost of the harmonica that Yolonda buys is $18.95. Yolonda's weekly allowance is $8.00 and Andrew's is $3.00. Make a chart by dividing your paper into columns labeled "Instrument," "Cost," "Weeks for Yolonda," "Weeks for Andrew," "Weeks for Both Children." Then write "harmonica" and "$18.95" in the appropriate columns and calculate the number of weeks each child would need to save to buy the harmonica. Calculate how many weeks it would take if they combined their allowances. Finally, find five other musical instruments advertised in a newspaper. Add them to the chart and complete the calculations.

5. Writing

Recognizing her daughter's potential, Josie Blue tells Yolonda that she can become a lawyer, judge, or doctor, but Yolonda pictures herself as a police officer like her dad. Obtain a copy of page 60 from your teacher. Fill in the job application as if you were Yolonda.

6. Science

Andrew expresses his feelings by playing an incredible range of *pitch,* the highness or lowness of sound, on his harmonica. Conduct an experiment testing pitch. Gather a spoon and five drinking glasses. Hypothesize about how different amounts of water in each glass will affect the sound produced when the glass is tapped with the spoon. Pour different amounts of water into each glass and test your hypothesis. Write your conclusions and then adjust each jar's water level until you can play a recognizable tune on the glasses.

Yolonda's Genius

Independent Contract

Name:_____ Number of activities to be completed: _____

 Language Arts — 7.

Before confronting the Dudes on Asphalt Hill, Yolonda plans her strategy carefully. She overpowers the three gang members but doesn't try to hurt them. Instead, Yolonda warns them not to bother her brother again. She could have taken the opportunity to lecture the Dudes on the importance of a good education and the harmful effects of substance abuse. Plan and write a monologue from Yolonda's point of view in which you lecture the Dudes about these issues. Then, taking on the role of Yolonda, act out the scene for your class.

 Research — 8.

Yolonda is convinced that Andrew is a musical *prodigy,* or a highly talented child. Mozart, a child prodigy, and many other great musicians are mentioned in *Yolonda's Genius*. Research five of the musicians listed below. Using the five *w's* (who, what, when, where, and why), write a brief summary about each musician on a separate sheet of paper. Publish your work in a booklet and decorate it with music symbols.

Frédéric Chopin	Wolfgang Mozart	B. B. King
Nat "King" Cole	Fontella Bass	Sarah Vaughan
Stevie Ray Vaughan	Eubie Blake	Richard Wagner

 Science — 9.

Yolonda longed to be good at double Dutch. Develop your jump-roping skills during your free time. Keep count of your jumps and create a bar graph to record your progress. Time yourself to find out how fast you jump and work to increase your speed. Try other jump-roping tricks like crossovers and double jumping. To find out more about this sport, write to the USAJRF® (United States Amateur Jump Rope Federation), P.O. Box 569, Huntsville, TX 77342 or visit http://www.usajrf.org (current as of October, 2000). Then teach a friend how to jump rope.

 Language Arts — 10.

Chicago hadn't changed much when Yolonda and her family returned to visit Aunt Tiny. What is it like today? Are there still large music festivals at Grant Park? Visit Chicago's Web site at http://www.ci.chi.il.us (current as of October, 2000). Using the online map, geography facts, points of interest, and other valuable information about the city, develop a trifold travel brochure. Make sure your brochure is informative, colorful, and eye-catching.

 Music — 11.

Andrew is fascinated by musical instruments. Search through magazines and cut out pictures of various musical instruments. Draw and cut out music symbols from construction paper. Glue the instrument pictures to the construction paper shapes. On the back of each shape, write the instrument's name and classification (woodwind, brass, stringed, percussion, or keyboard). Use reference materials to help you. Survey your classmates to find out which instruments they play. Illustrate the data you collect as a pictograph and glue it to a wire hanger. Suspend the instrument pictures from it with string to create a musical mobile.

 Writing — 12.

Yolonda's Genius is written from an *omniscient* point of view. The storyteller knows every detail, including the characters' thoughts and actions. *First person* is another point of view in which a character in the story seems to be telling the reader what is happening. Choose an episode from the book, such as the attack on Andrew by the Dudes in chapter 7 or the shopping trip to purchase the harmonica in chapter 9. Think about how the episode would be different if it were told in the first person. Then rewrite the events in the first person as though Andrew, Shirley Piper, or Yolonda's mother is speaking.

Room With a View

Directions: The panes at the top of the window contain details about Yolonda's life in Chicago and her life in Grand River. Locate each detail in the book and write its corresponding page number on each moon. Look back through the book to find additional details about the two cities. Write one detail in each of the lower panes and its corresponding page number on the star. Then color the window panes with details about Chicago yellow and those about Grand River blue.

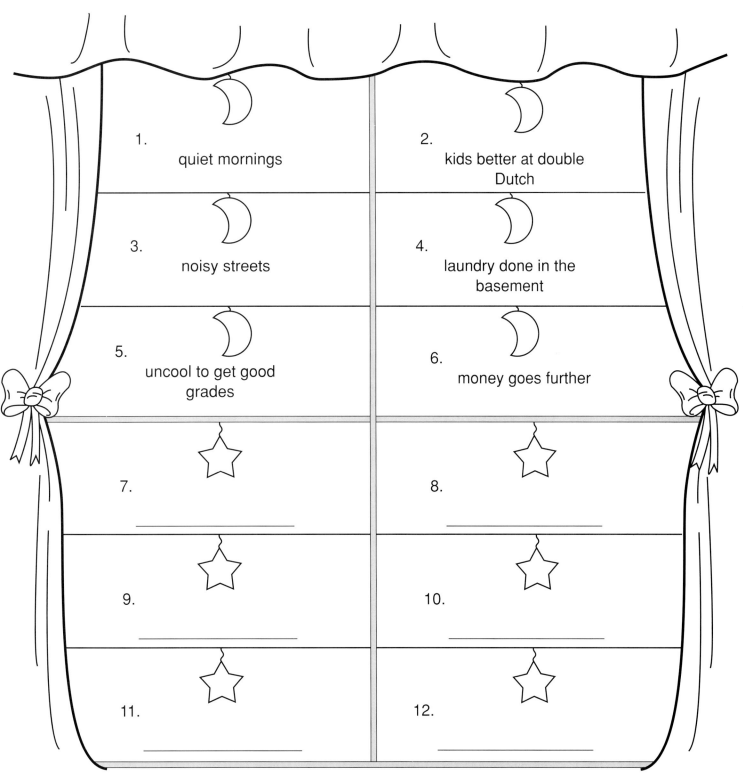

1. quiet mornings

2. kids better at double Dutch

3. noisy streets

4. laundry done in the basement

5. uncool to get good grades

6. money goes further

7. _____

8. _____

9. _____

10. _____

11. _____

12. _____

Note to the teacher: Use with activity #2 on page 57.

Name_____

Directions: Think about how badly Yolonda wants to become a police officer. Then complete the following junior police officer application as if you were her.

Junior Police Officer Application

Name: _____

Date: _____

Position desired: _____

Are you a citizen of the United States? _____

Are you below the age of 18? _____

What are your future educational goals? _____

_____

_____

References: Provide the names of two people who can give information regarding your ability to perform this job.

1. _____

2. _____

What special qualifications or skills do you have that would help you with this position?

_____

_____

In a complete paragraph, explain why you want to become a junior police officer.

_____

_____

_____

_____

_____

_____

_____

_____

_____

_____

Note to the teacher: Use with activity #5 on page 57.

Reach Into the Real World With Realistic Fiction

Get ready to laugh, cry, get mad, feel happy, and have fun
with this collection of realistic fiction novels.

Bloomability by Sharon Creech • Dinnie's father is always moving the family in search of opportunities. Then, one day, Dinnie's aunt and uncle whisk her away to an international school in Switzerland. Will this be the home she's always dreamed about?

Dear Mr. Henshaw by Beverly Cleary • The assignment is to write an author, ask him questions, and then write a report about him. Leigh Botts chooses Mr. Henshaw and writes him a series of letters. Mr. Henshaw writes back with some humorous answers and good advice.

The Girls' Revenge by Phyllis Reynolds Naylor • Ever since the Malloy sisters moved into the Hatford brothers' best friends' house for the year, the brothers have been playing tricks on them. Now it is Caroline Malloy's chance to get back at Wally Hatford, but her plan backfires and it looks like the Hatfords may win the war after all.

Just Juice by Karen Hesse • Juice Faulstich lives with her mom, dad, and four sisters. She has a hard time in school when she goes. Unfortunately, the family has hit hard times and now they may have to pay $1,000 because Juice hasn't been going to school.

The Landry News by Andrew Clements • Cara Landry has done it again. She's in a new school and already her journalistic skills have gotten her into trouble. Her newspaper features articles that, while true, often hurt others' feelings. This time the one who gets hurt is her teacher.

Lolo and Red-Legs by Kirk Reeve • Isidoro "Lolo" Garcia lives in Los Angeles, California. One day he finds a tarantula and decides to capture it and keep it as a pet. Red-Legs turns out to be a great pet, until somebody steals or kills her. Now Lolo must find out if Red-Legs is alive or dead.

Me, Mop, and the Moondance Kid by Walter Dean Myers • T. J. Walker, his friend Mop, and his little brother Moondance grew up together in the same orphanage. T. J. and his brother have been adopted, but Mop hasn't and the orphanage is going to close soon. What will happen to Mop if she doesn't get adopted? What will happen to their friendship?

Mick Harte Was Here by Barbara Park • Phoebe's younger brother, Mick, has been killed in a bicycle accident. She deals with this loss by telling stories of their growing up together and the wacky things he used to do, such as getting his head stuck in a wrought-iron fence and putting a ceramic eye in his mom's defrosted chicken.

One Thing I'm Good At by Karen Lynn Williams • Julie Dorinsky is having a hard time at school, at home, and with her friends. Ever since her dad had a heart attack, nothing seems to be going right and Julie feels like she isn't good at anything.

The Silver Balloon by Susan Bonners • Can a simple index card tied to a balloon lead Gregory to a new friend? He hopes so, but when he finds out his pen pal is an adult, Gregory worries that they won't be able to write each other anymore.

The Trouble With Tuck by Theodore Taylor • Friar Tuck has belonged to Helen since she was nine years old. Now that her dog is going blind she doesn't know what to do for him. She has to help him, and she will—as soon as she figures out how.

The War With Grandpa by Robert Kimmel Smith • When Grandpa moves in and takes over Peter's room, war is declared. Peter wants his room back and will stop at nothing to get it back. But this time, he may have gone too far.

Answer Keys

Page 16
1. Sport
2. Franca
3. Harriet's mother
4. Miss Whitehead
5. Pinky Whitehead
6. Janie

Page 20
Students' responses will vary. Accept all reasonable responses.

Page 21
Students' responses will vary. Accept all reasonable responses. Possible responses are listed below.

1. The book doesn't mention any dates; it only states seasons.
   The narrator talks as if the events happened a long time ago.
2. The book says that if everyone who claimed to have seen Maniac the first day he came to town really saw him, there would have been 10,000 people waiting for him at the town limits.
   The whole town was buzzing about Maniac Magee.
3. At the beginning of the book, there is a list of different things people say about Maniac Magee.
   The book says that school girls jump rope and chant about Maniac's deeds.
4. Maniac treated everyone fairly regardless of the color of their skin.
   Aunt Dot and Uncle Dan were extremely hateful.
5. The book starts by saying that Maniac was born in a dump, but this did not really happen.
   The book says that Maniac's stomach is a cereal box, but that's not true.
6. This book teaches that everyone is the same, regardless of the color of their skin.
   This book teaches that if you treat people well, they will usually treat you well in return.

Page 26

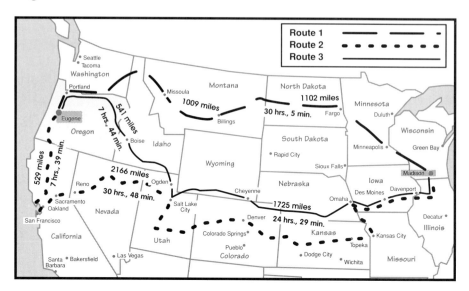

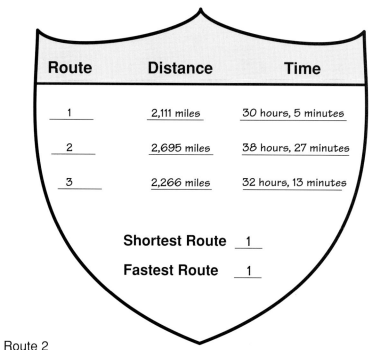

Route	Distance	Time
1	2,111 miles	30 hours, 5 minutes
2	2,695 miles	38 hours, 27 minutes
3	2,266 miles	32 hours, 13 minutes

Shortest Route 1

Fastest Route 1

6. Route 2
7. Route 1
8. Students' responses will vary.

Page 30

1. Marty's dad
2. Marty
3. Marty's dad
4. Marty's ma
5. Judd
6. Marty
7. Mrs. Howard
8. Marty's ma
9. Marty's ma
10. Doc Murphy
11. Marty's dad
12. Dara Lynn
13. David
14. Judd
15. Marty's dad
16. Judd

Page numbers will vary depending on the book version.

Page 31

Students' responses will vary. Accept all reasonable responses.

Page 36

Students' responses will vary. Accept all reasonable responses.

Page 37

1. Allegheny
2. Blue Ridge
3. sugar maple
4. Mountain
5. Charleston
6. coal
7. Forests
8. Ohio River
   Montani Semper Liberi

Page 38

Students' responses will vary. Accept all reasonable responses.

Page 42

Students' responses will vary. Possible responses are listed below.

Nadia's Life Before the Divorce
lived with both parents
celebrated holidays with both parents
had good friends in Florida

Things That Have Stayed the Same
has a dog named Ginger
is concerned about the Florida turtles
dad is still a nervous person

Nadia's Life After the Divorce
lives with her mom in New York
dad lives in a swinging singles apartment complex
has to divide her time between her parents
friends in Florida are not as much fun as they used to be

Page 47

Sal's goal is to reach Idaho before her mother's birthday. Answers may vary but should refer to problems Sal has adjusting to the permanent loss of her mother.

Phoebe's goal is to find out where her mother is and why she left. Answers may vary but should refer to problems Phoebe has adjusting to her mother's disappearance.

Sal's mother's goal is to find out who she really is. Answers may vary but should refer to her having to overcome the loss of her baby and her feelings about not being good.

Mrs. Winterbottom's goal is to remain respectable. Answers may vary but should refer to her trying to keep the existence of her son secret.

Ben's goal is to get Sal to like him. Answers may vary but should refer to his having to deal with his mother's mental illness.

Page 48

Students' responses will vary. Possible responses are listed below.

1. Phoebe's mother went away to find herself.
2. Phoebe thinks she can find her mother and bring her back.
3. Gram and Gramps want to go to Idaho to see Sal's mother.
4. Mrs. Cadaver wants to help Sal's father deal with his wife's death.
5. Phoebe was unkind to her mother before she left.
6. Ben drew his soul as a circle containing a maple leaf.
7. Phoebe feels jealous about having a brother.
8. Phoebe tries to make up reasons to explain why her mother left.
9. Sal's dad learns to deal with his loss by talking to Mrs. Cadaver about his wife.
10. Phoebe doesn't want her mother to care about someone other than her father.

Page 49

1. South Dakota, 6
2. Minnesota, 3
3. Idaho, 9
4. South Dakota, 5
5. Wisconsin, 2
6. Wyoming, 7
7. Idaho, 8
8. Ohio, 1
9. South Dakota, 4

Page 53

1. b
2. a
3. a
4. b
5. b
6. a
7. a
   Yingtao's team won 13 to 11.

Page 54

Student illustrations and meanings will vary. Possible meanings are listed below.

1. I am tone-deaf!
2. What's annoying you?
3. Everyone is watching you!
4. I really played my best.

Page 55

1. Students' responses will vary.
2. $3,180.60
   $3,600.00
   $3,384.00
   $3,390.00
3. In-the-Clouds Airline
4. Students' responses will vary.
5. Over-the-Treetops Airline
6. $419.40
7. Through-the-Air Airline, Skyline Flights
8. $3,420.00

Page 59

Page numbers will vary.
Yellow window panes: 2, 3, 5
Blue window panes: 1, 4, 6
Students' responses and colors will vary for 7–12.